This coloring book belongs to:

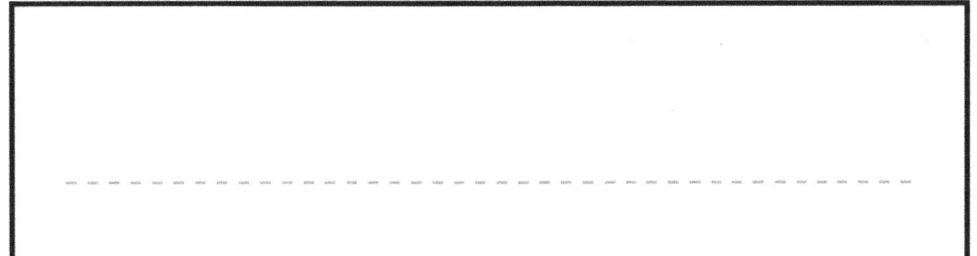

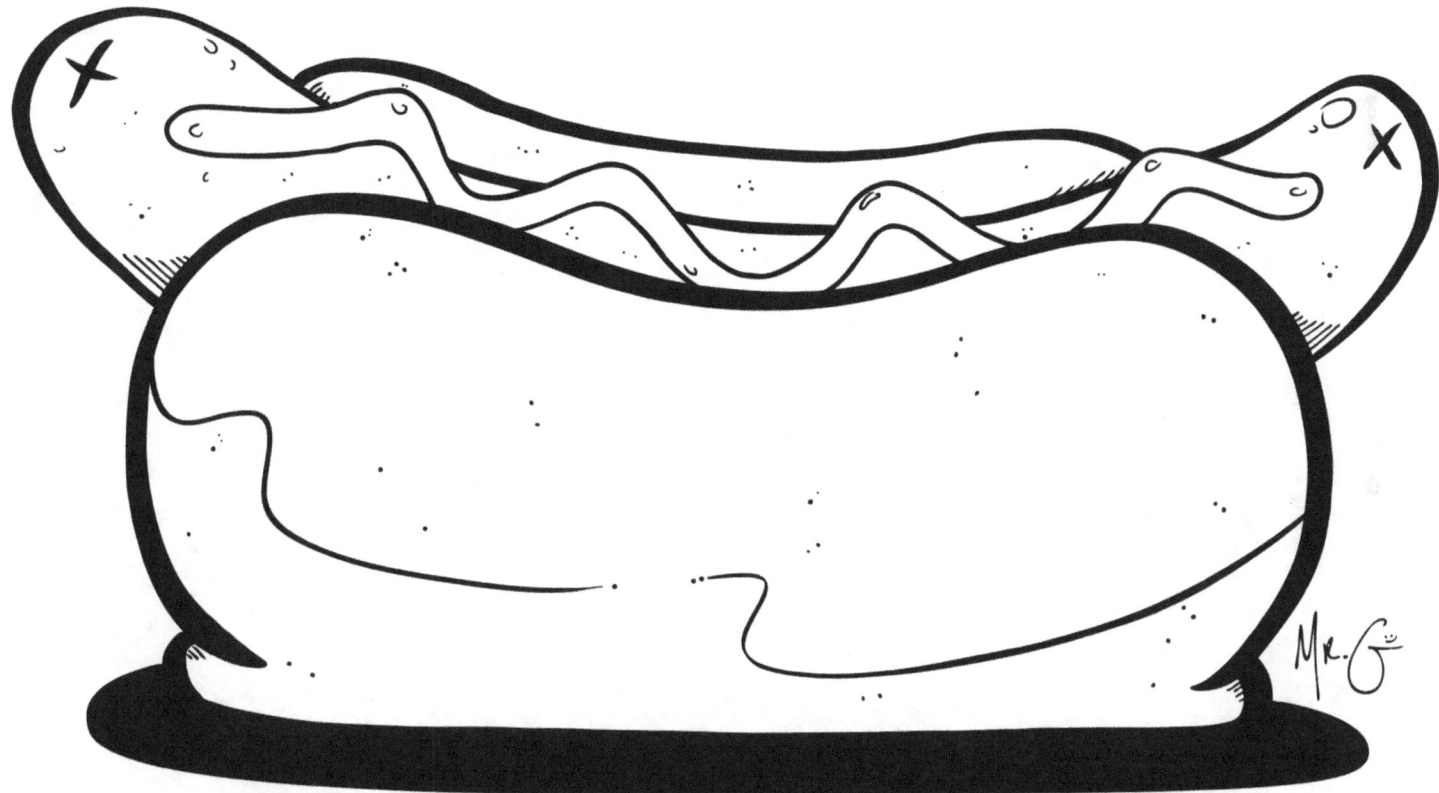

The Super Fantastical Flavor-Filled Food Coloring Book

(Volume One)

Illustrated By

Mr. Gray

Dedicated

to all the food lovers, ice cream eaters
and anyone dreaming about eating something
right now. Have fun coloring and remember…
do NOT eat the paper.

WELCOME

to The Super Fantastical Flavor-Filled Food Coloring Book Volume One!

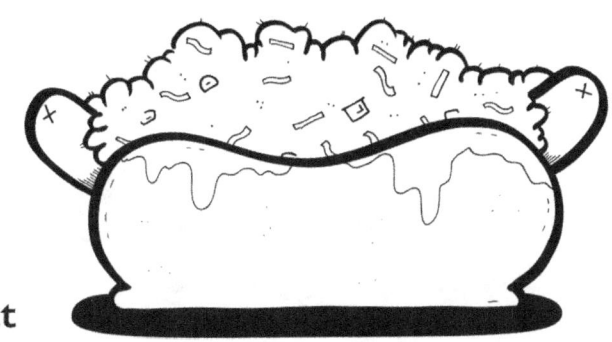

What's Inside?

1. FUN FACTS:

Each page has a fun and interesting fact about the food!

2. HIDDEN TREASURE:

Can you help Mr. Gray find all **8** of his missing cooking items?

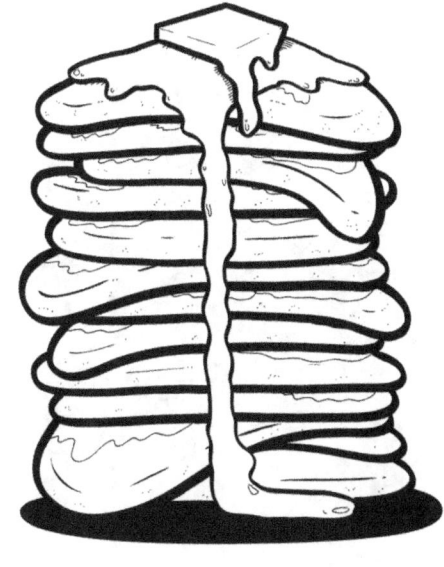

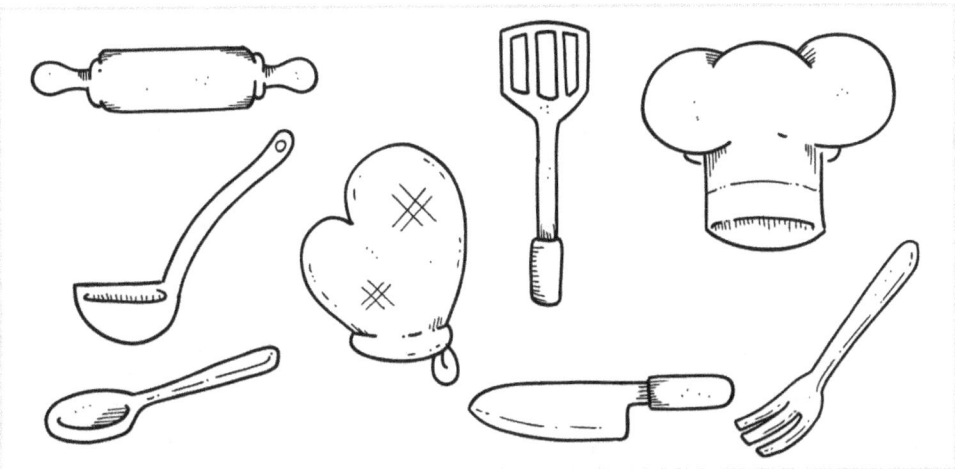

* The answer sheet can be found in back of the coloring book.

3. ONE-SIDED:

Each coloring page is printed on one side so you have the option to display your masterpiece and to color it with your favorite markers.

* **TIP:** Put a piece of paper behind the page you're coloring to prevent bleeding.

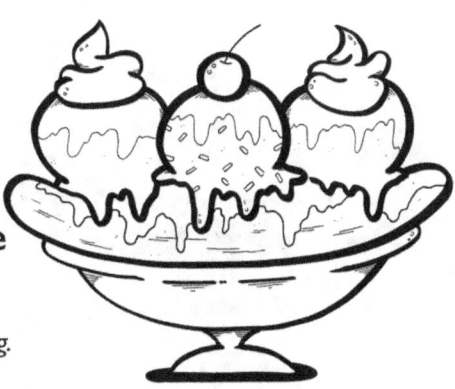

HAPPY COLORING!!

Did you know *Stichting Gouda Oogst*, a restaurant in the Netherlands, created the largest **Waffle** in the world?

It weighted 110 pounds!

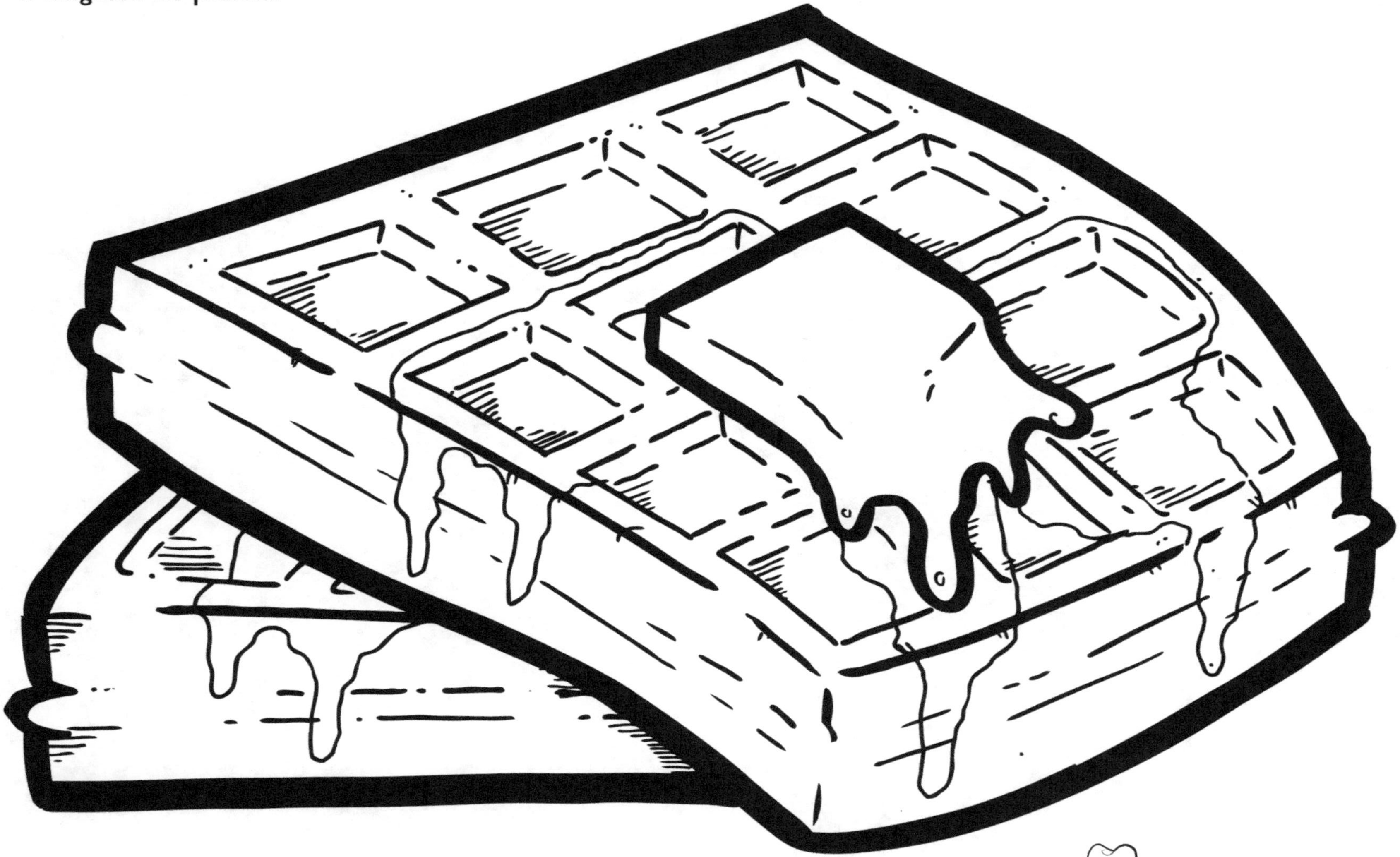

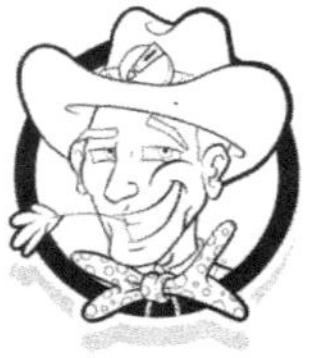

I wonder how many bottles of **syrup** you would need?

 Did you know **Cheese** could be produced using other varieties of milk such as camel milk?

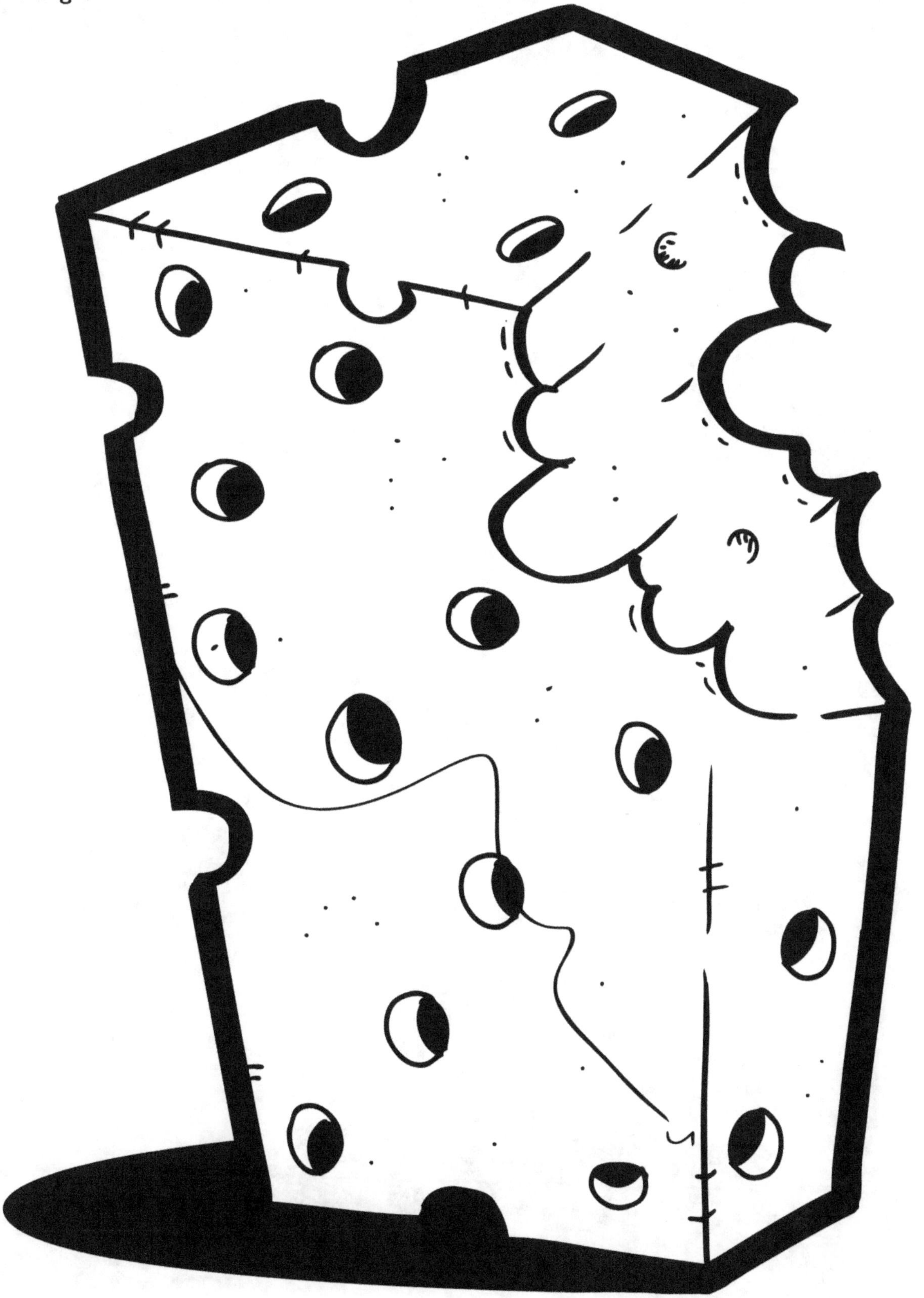

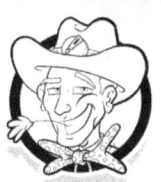 Now I know what's in those
Camel Humps! It's cheese!

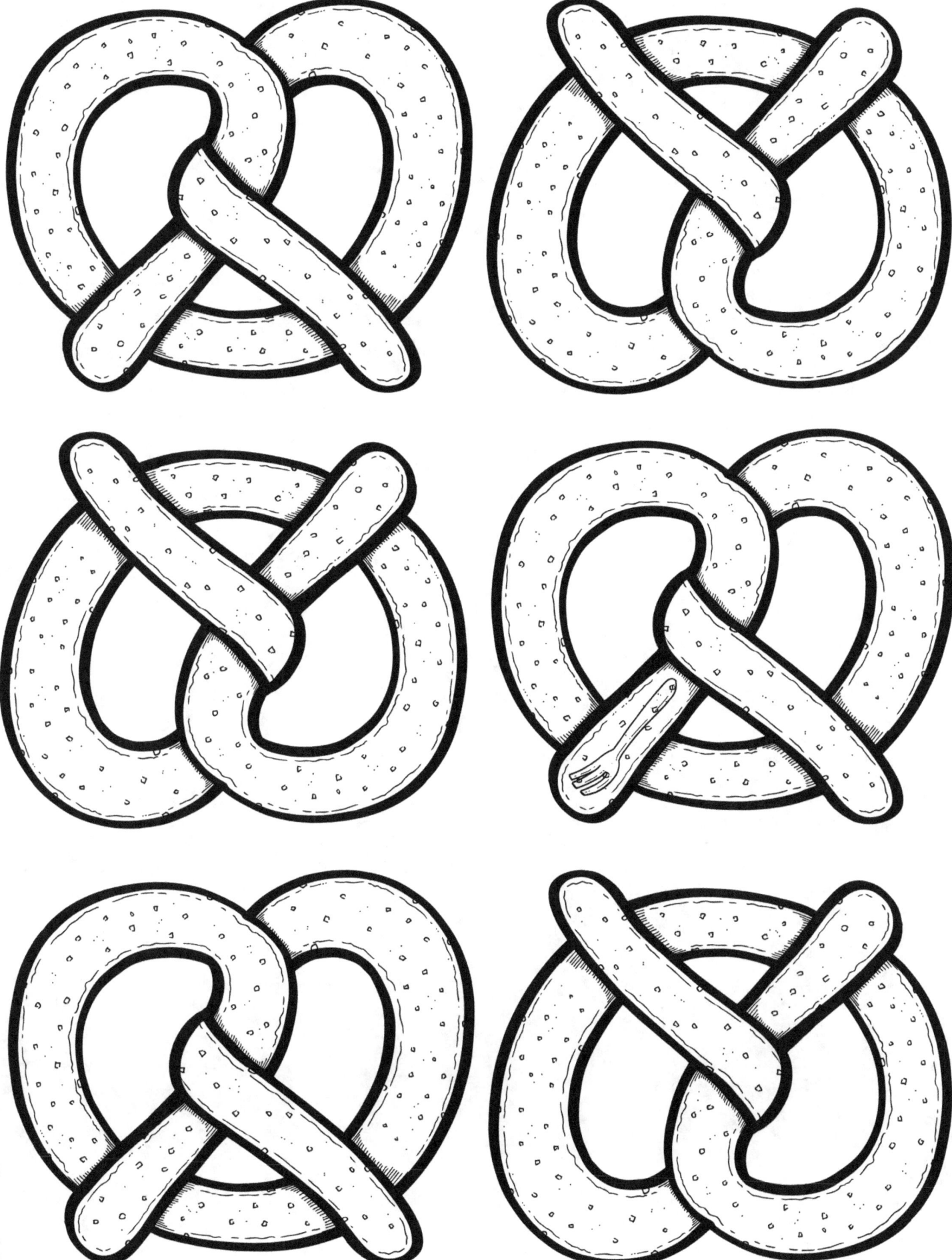

 Did you know the very first **Pizza Place** in the United States was *Lombardi's* in New York City in 1905?

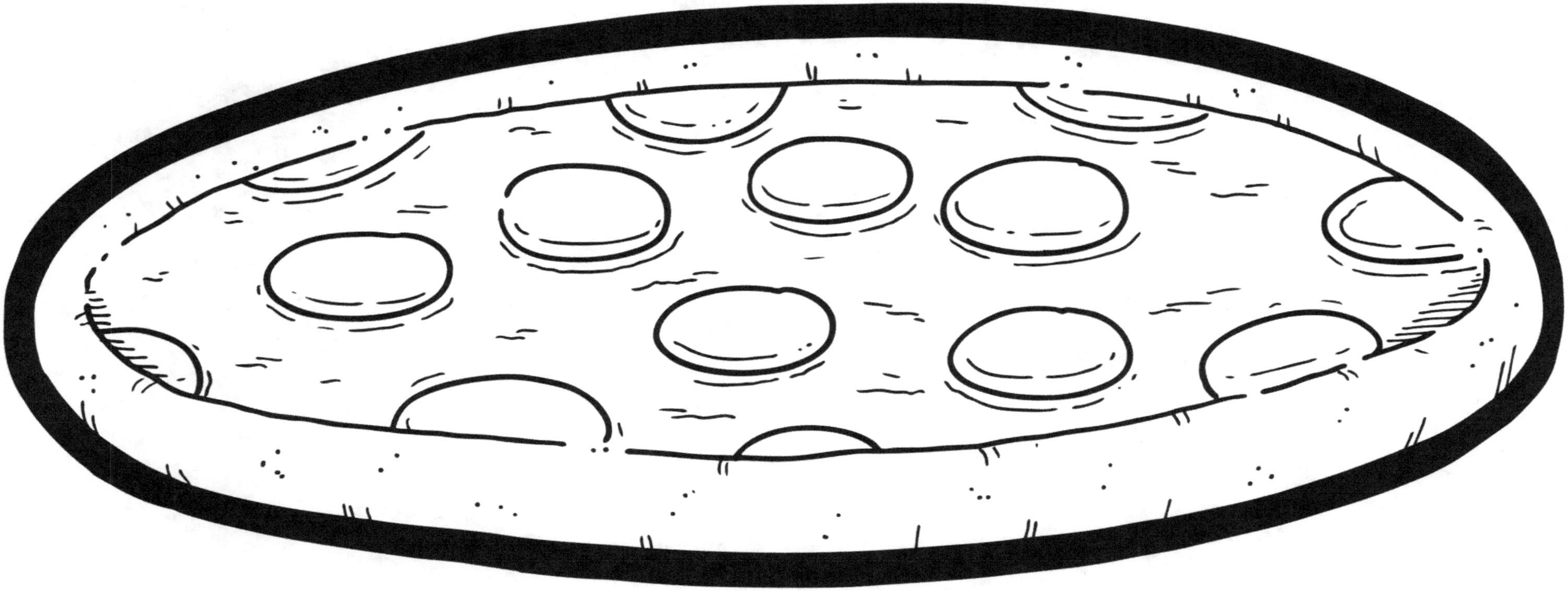

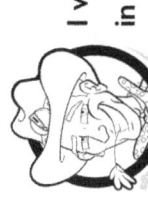 I wonder if they **delivered** in 30 minutes or less?

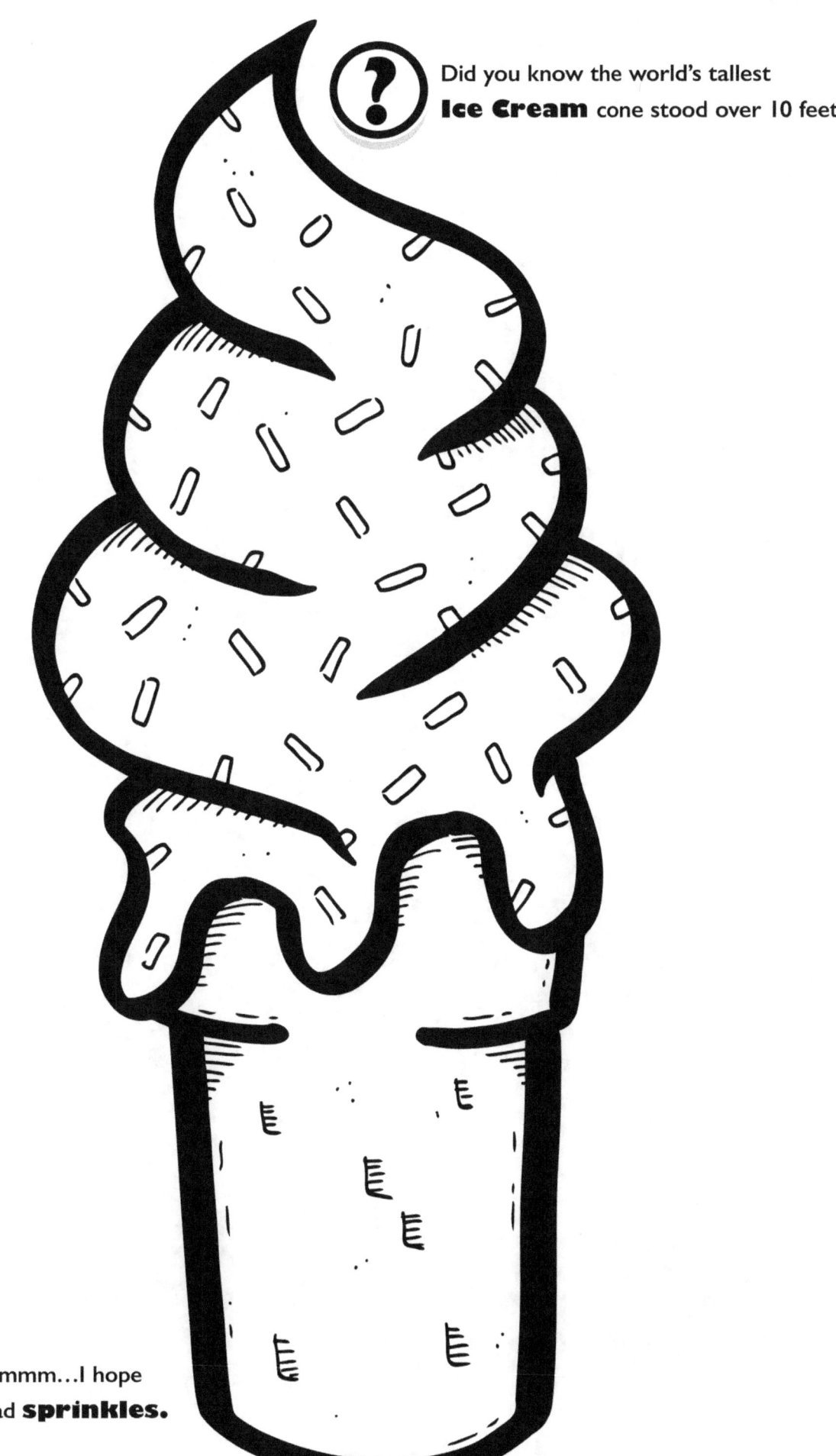

Did you know the world's tallest Ice Cream cone stood over 10 feet tall?

Mmmmm...I hope it had **sprinkles.**

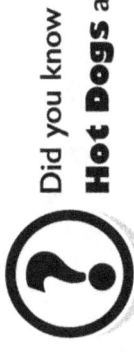

Did you know 7-11 sells over 100 million **Hot Dogs** a year in North America?

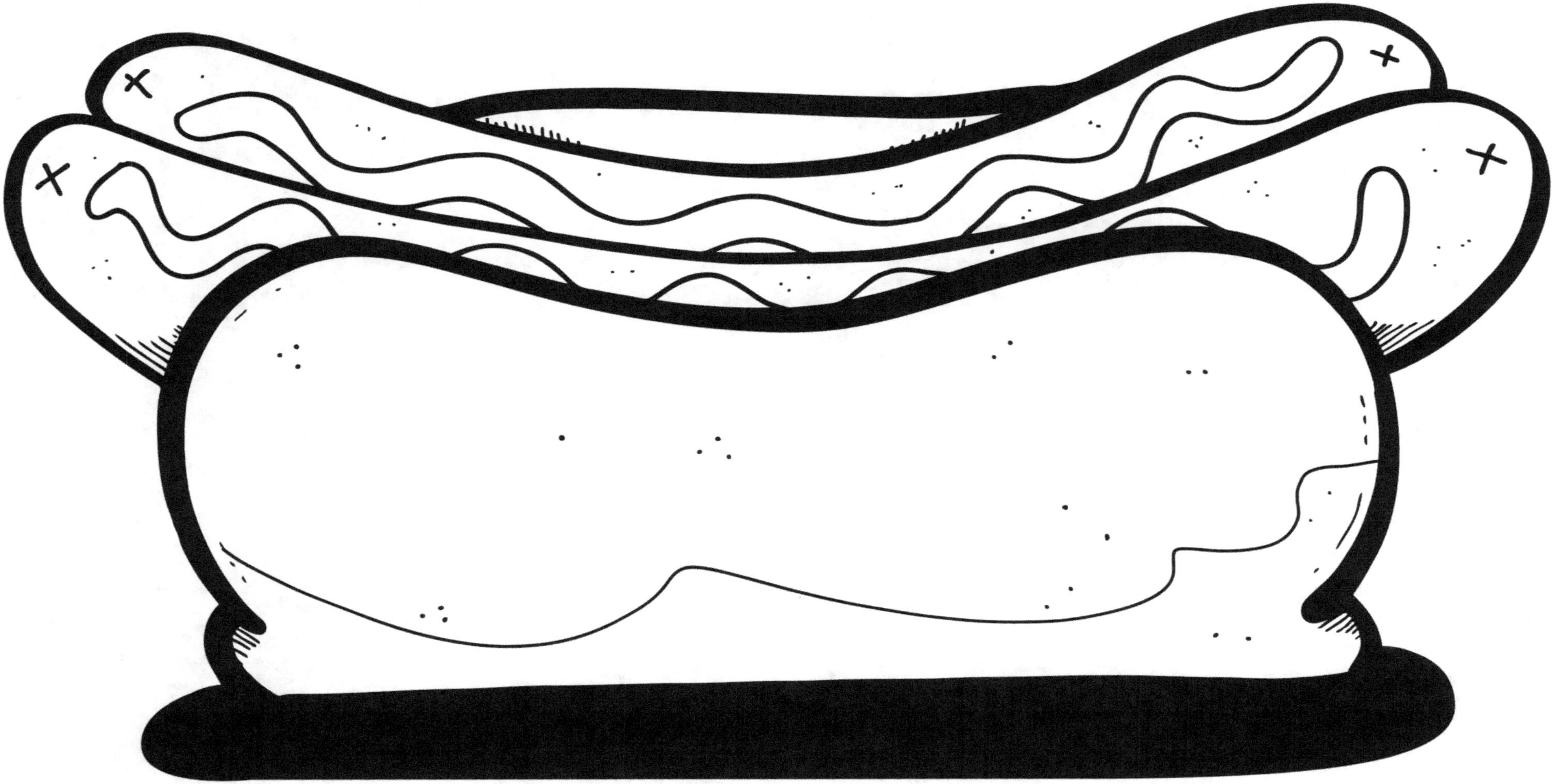

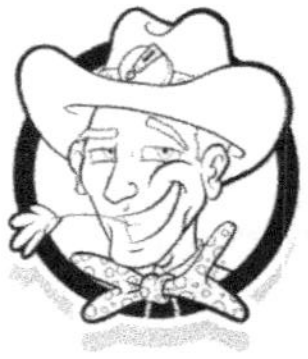

I wonder how many of those are covered in **chili?**

Did you know there is a **Hamburger** Hall of Fame in Seymour, Wisconsin?

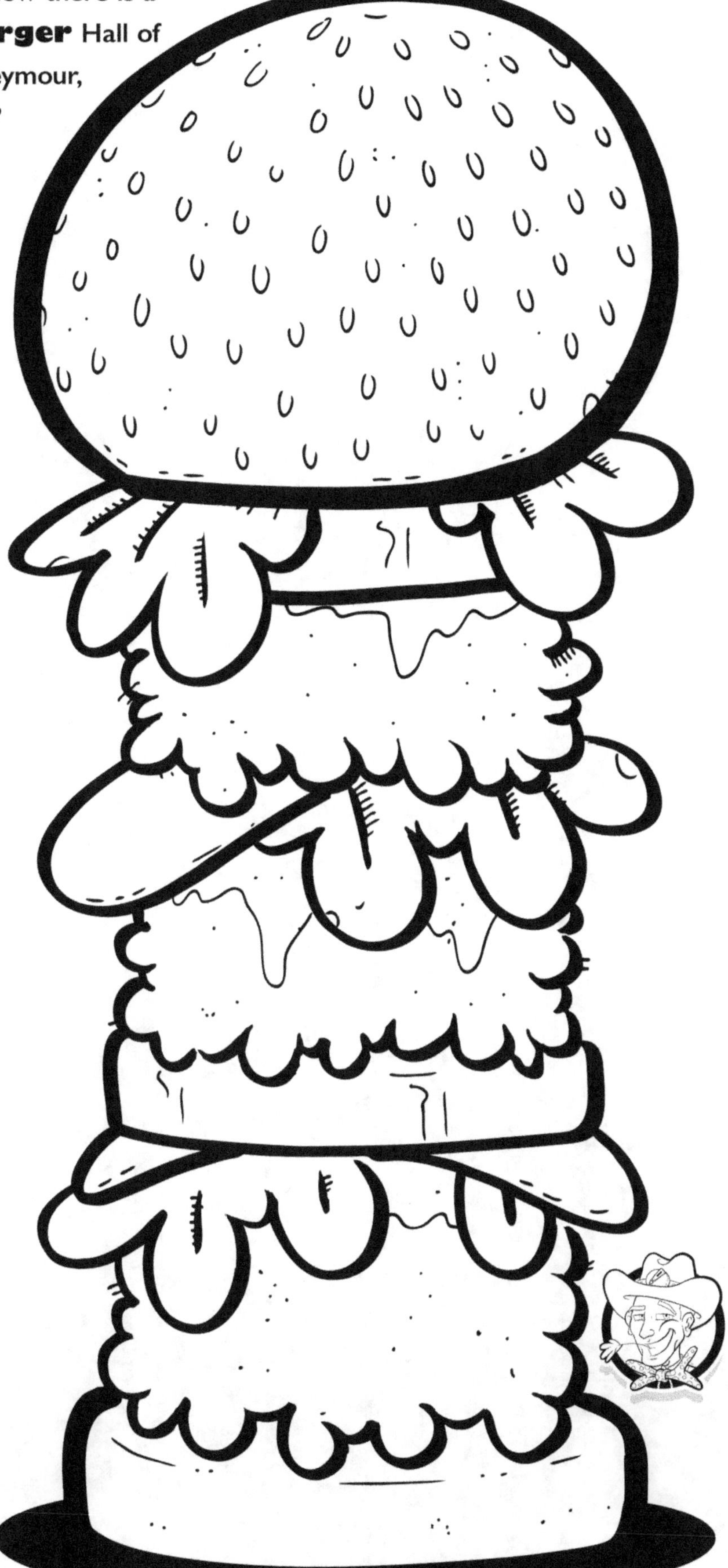

Skip Disneyland and go to the Hamburger Hall of Fame! Ha-ha

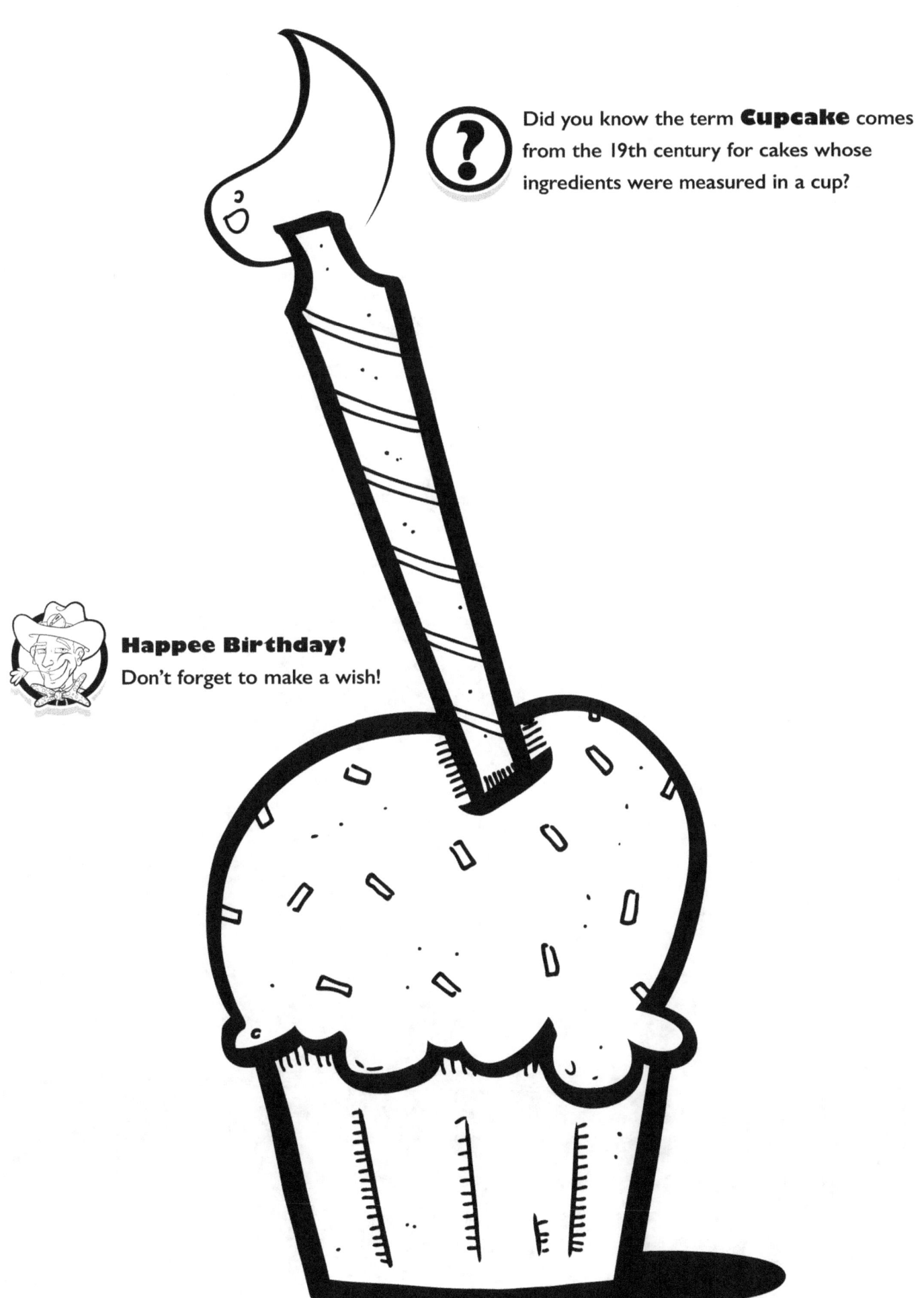

Did you know the term **Cupcake** comes from the 19th century for cakes whose ingredients were measured in a cup?

Happee Birthday!
Don't forget to make a wish!

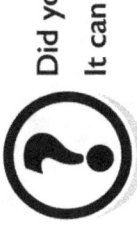

Did you know **Doughnut** is the more traditional spelling?

It can also be spelled as 'donut.'

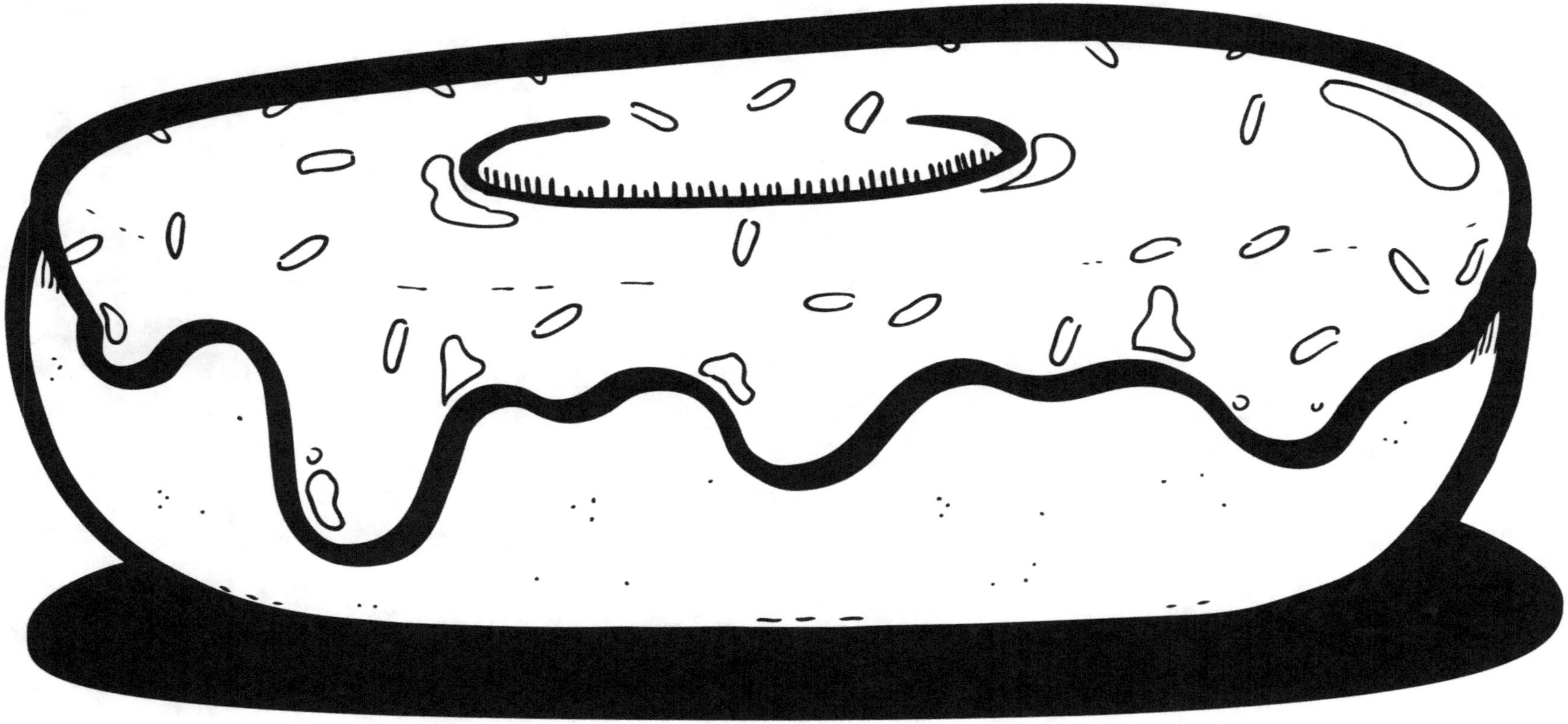

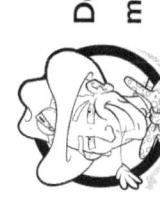

Doughnut, donuts...just give me glaze and **sprinkles.**

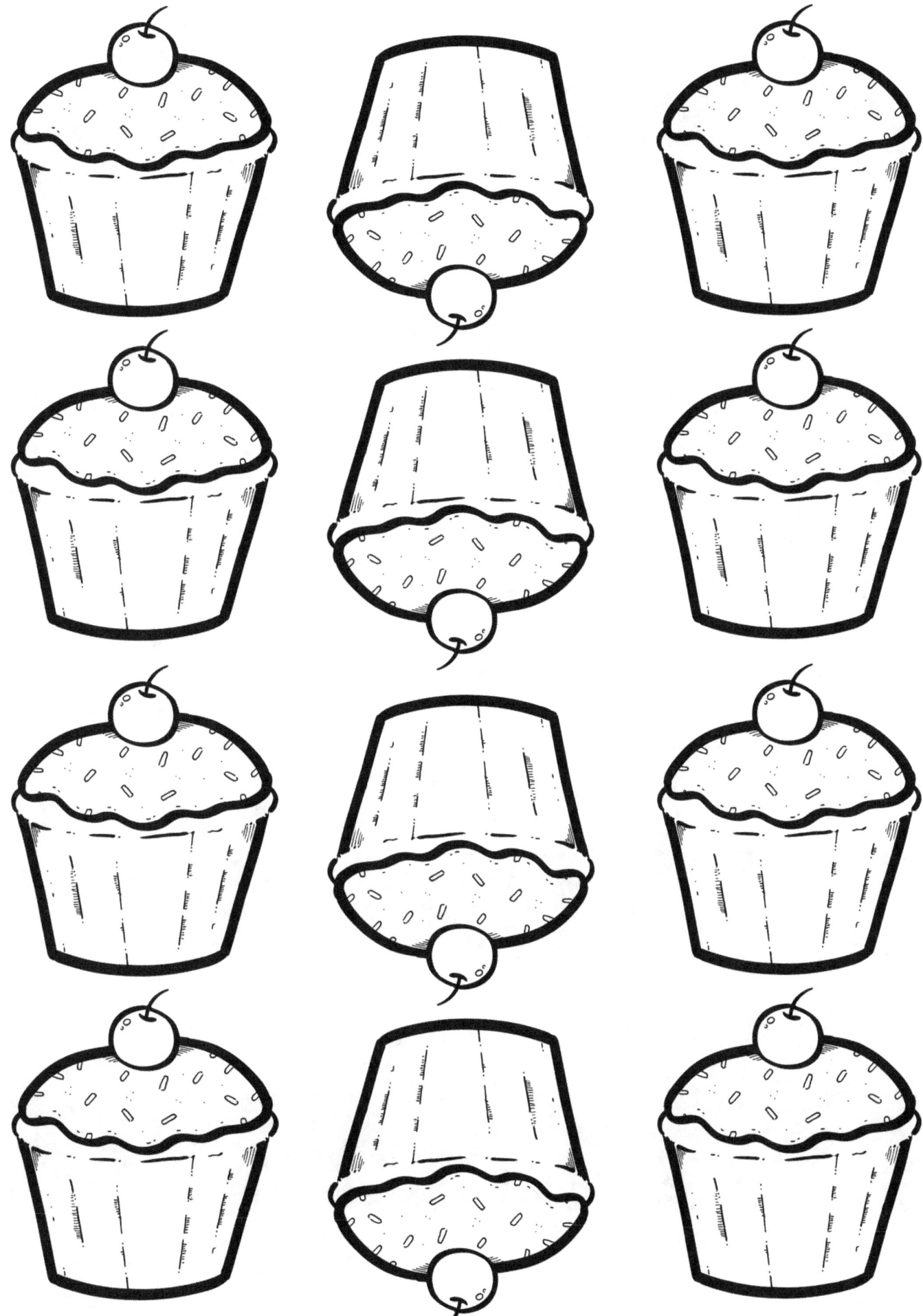

Did you know **Maize** is the 2nd largest crop in the world?

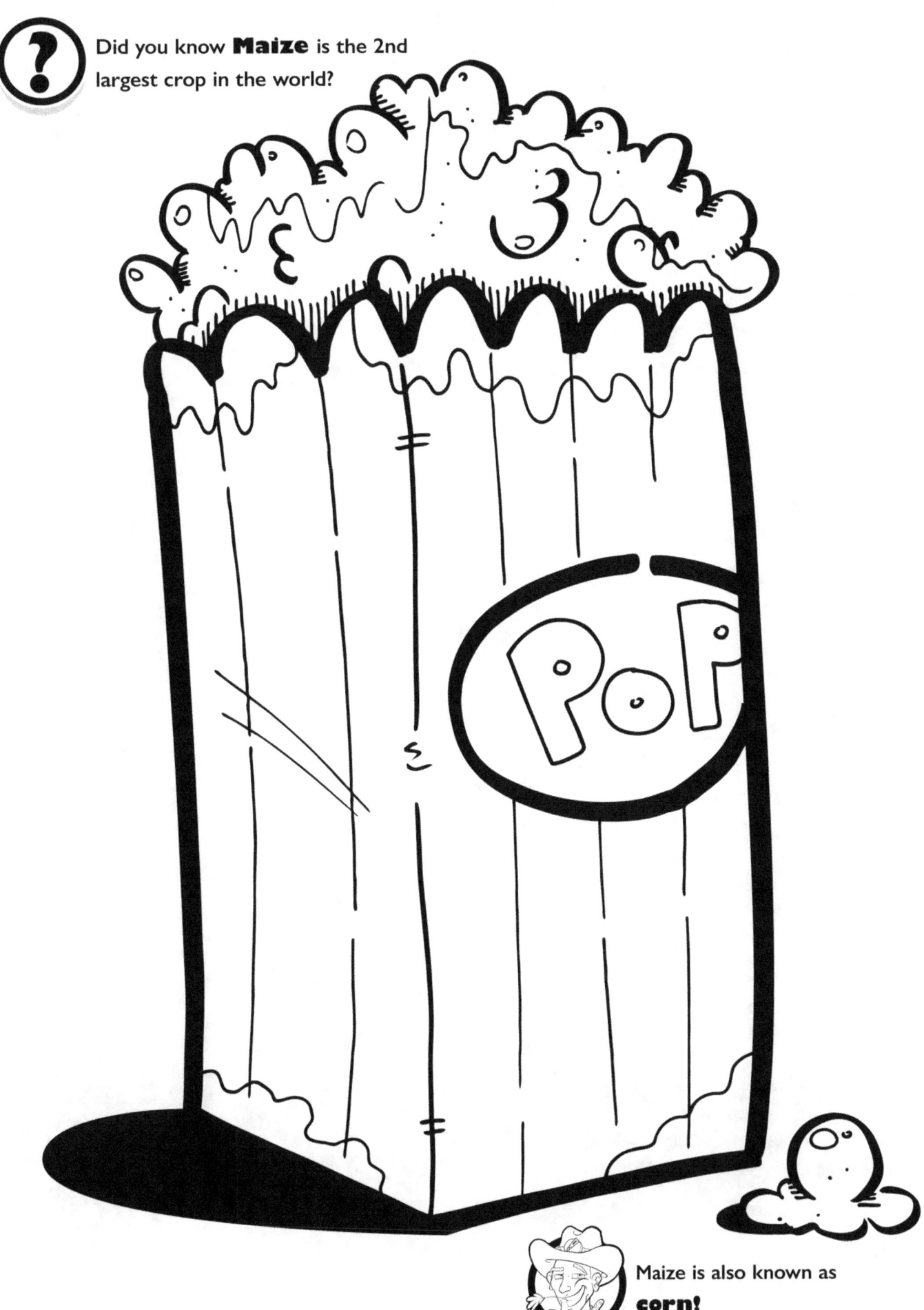

Maize is also known as **corn!**

 Did you know China produces an estimated 45 billion pairs of disposable **Chopsticks** every year?

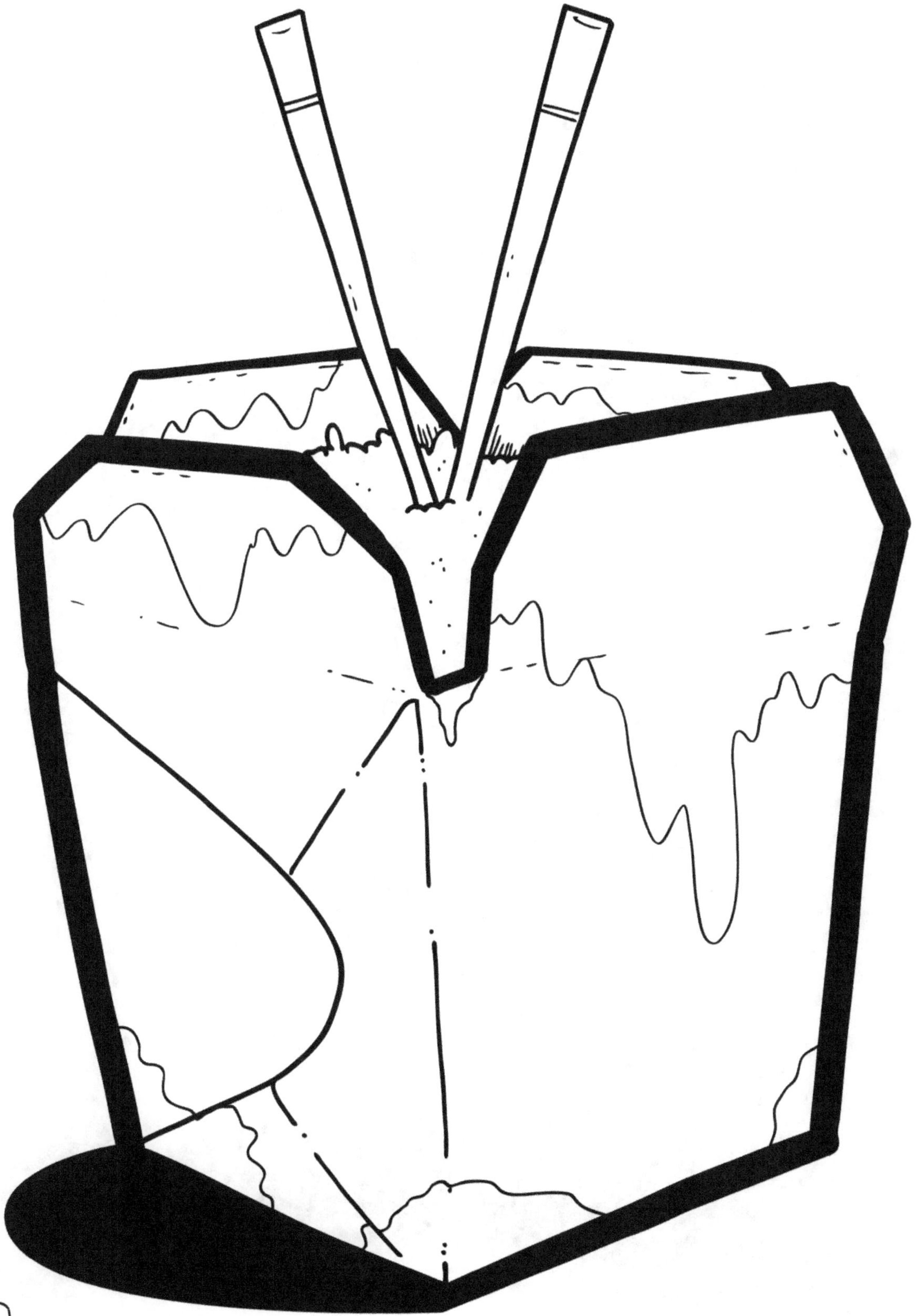

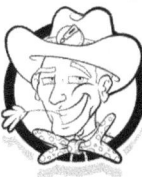 **Whoa**...that is a lot of chopsticks.

Did you know one ear of **corn** contains around 800 kernels?

Who **counted** all those kernels?

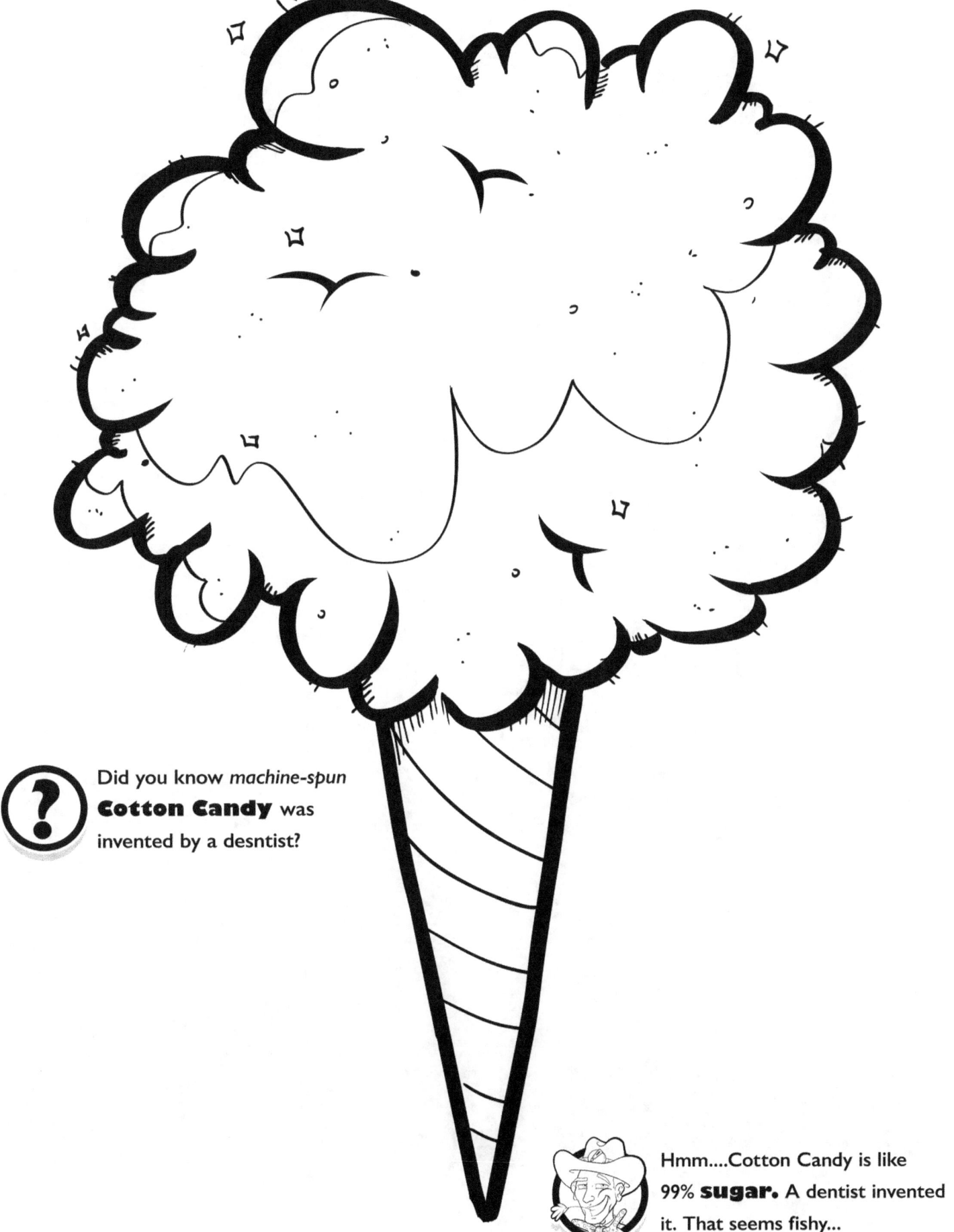

? Did you know *machine-spun* **Cotton Candy** was invented by a desntist?

Hmm....Cotton Candy is like 99% **sugar.** A dentist invented it. That seems fishy...

 Did you know the origin of **French Fries** can be traced back to Belgium?

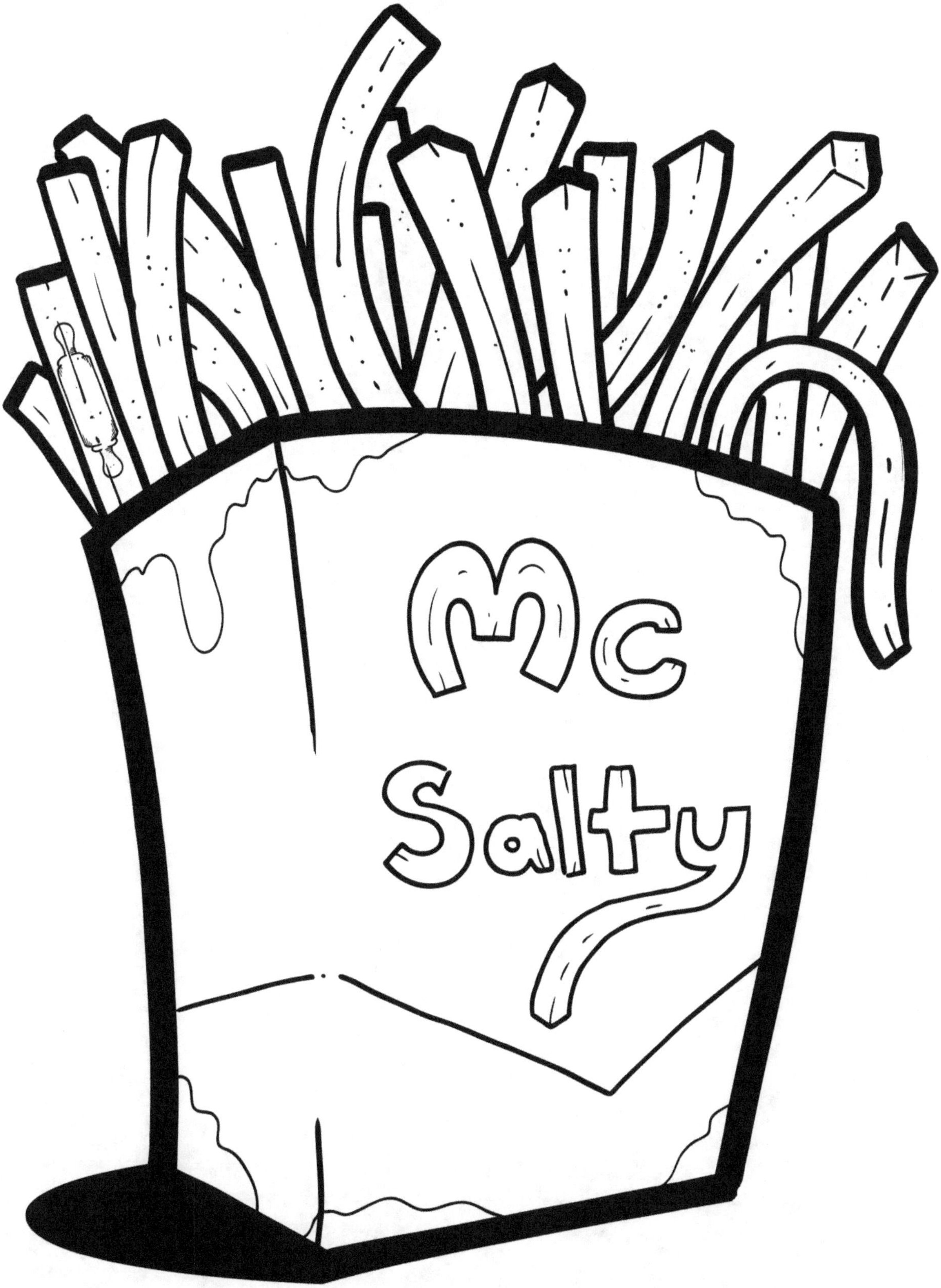

Mc Salty

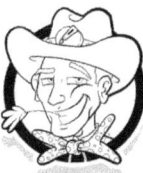 Then why don't we call them **Belgium Fries?**

? Did you know July is **National Blueberry Month** in the United States?

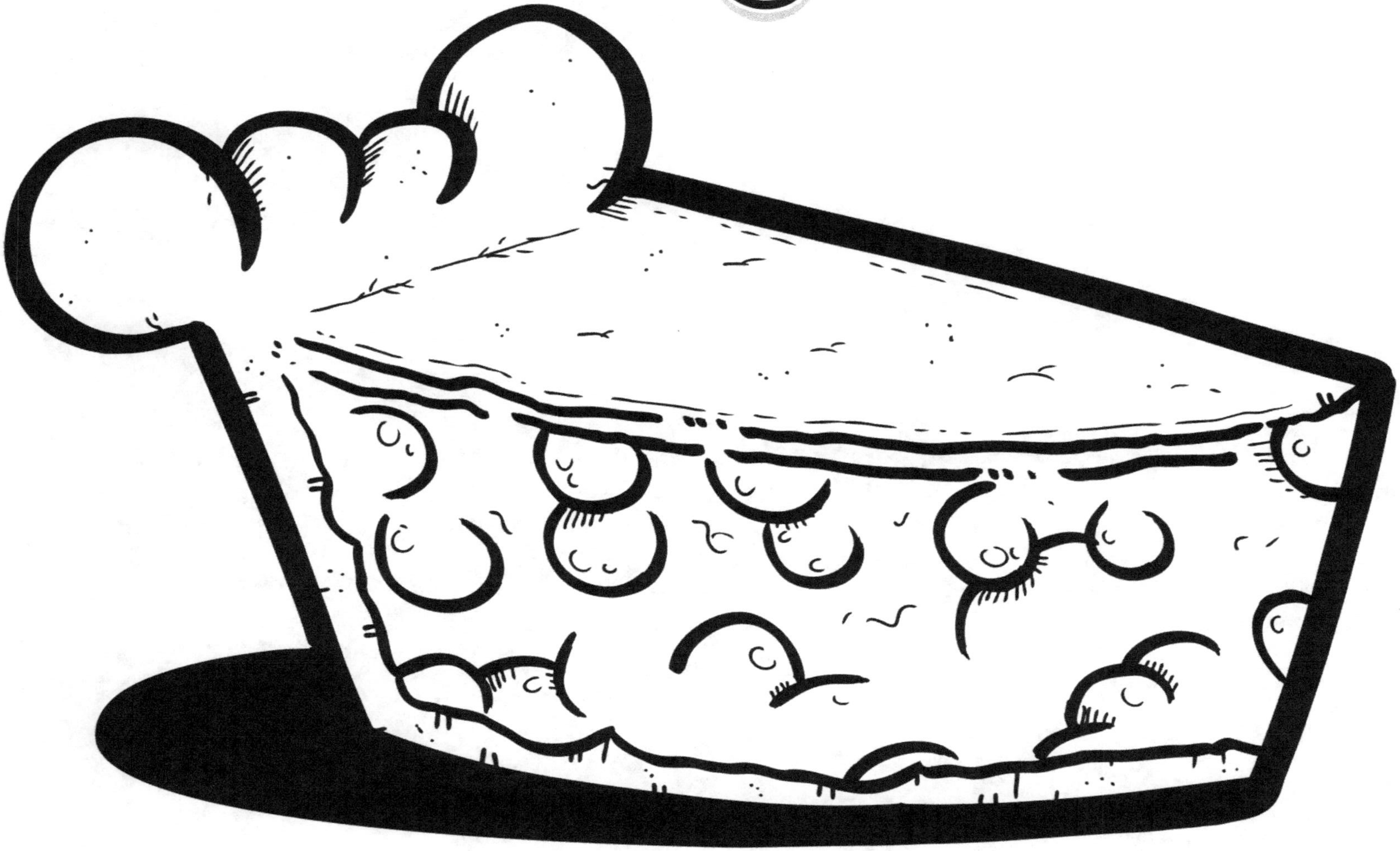

I wonder how many **blueberries** you can fit inside one pie?

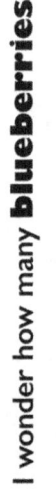

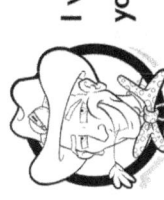

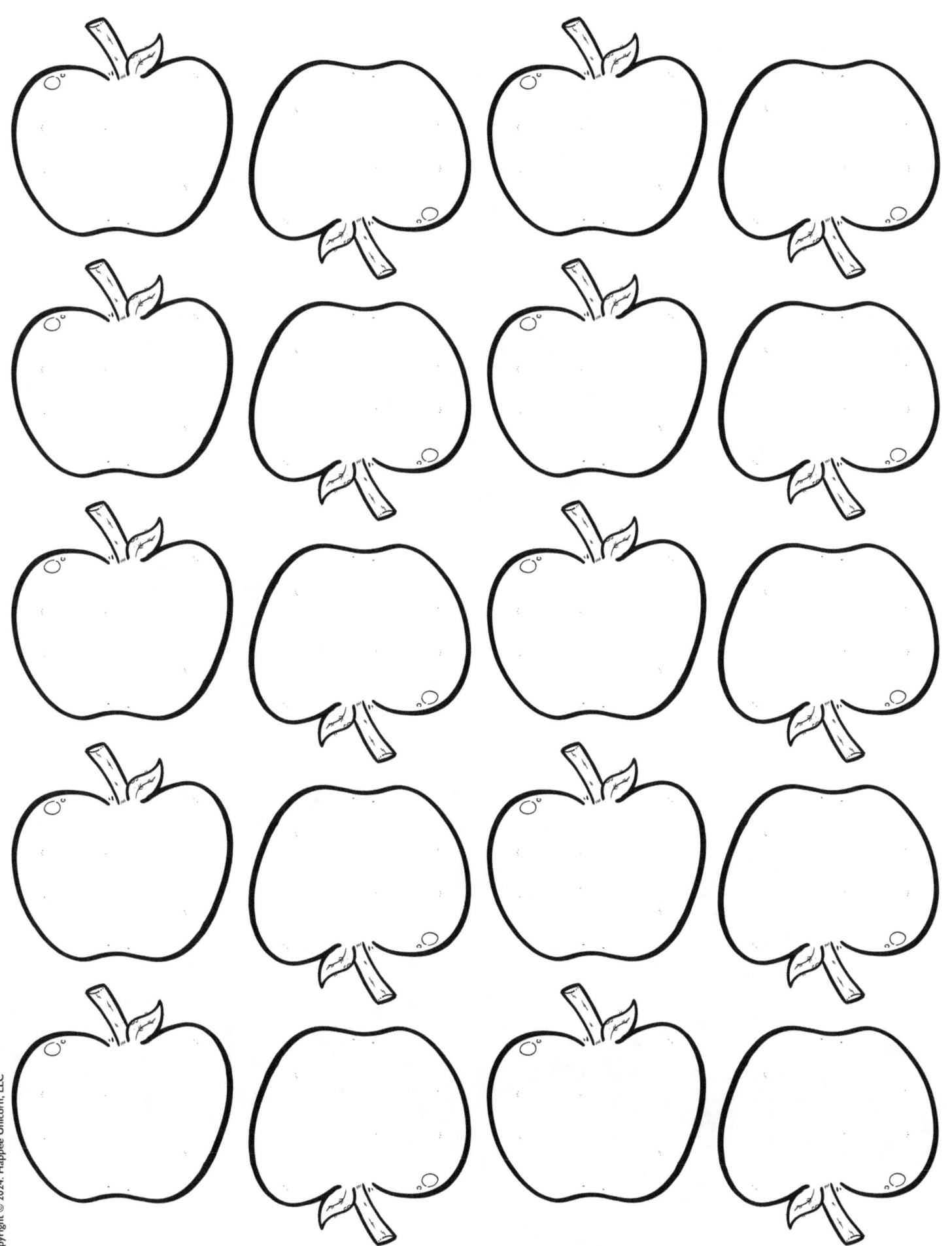

 Did you know California produces the most **Ice Cream** each year in the United States?

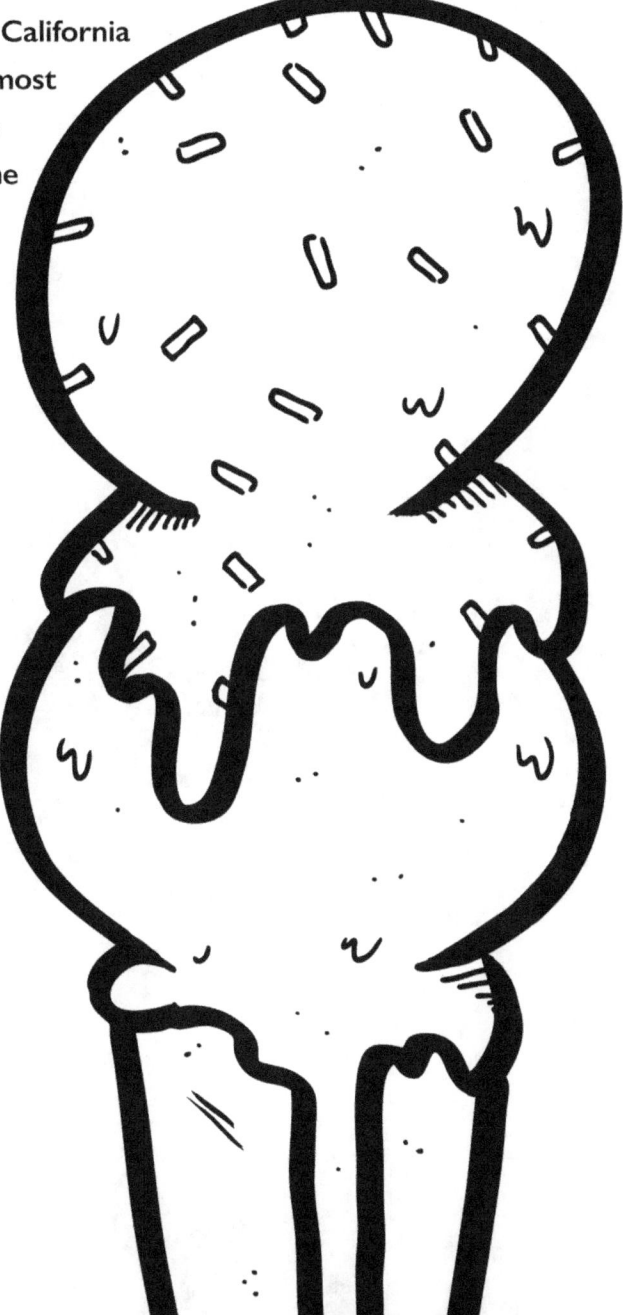

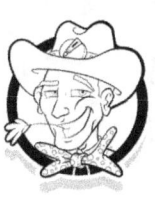 Yeah, because that's me, **eating** it all.

Did you know that an **Avocado** is actually a fruit?

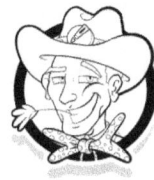 I like to think **Guacamole** is Avocado's alter ego.

? Did you know **Ham** comes from the upper part of a pig's leg?

My favorite is **honey glazed ham!**

 Did you know **Cupcakes** are known as fairy cakes in Great Britain?

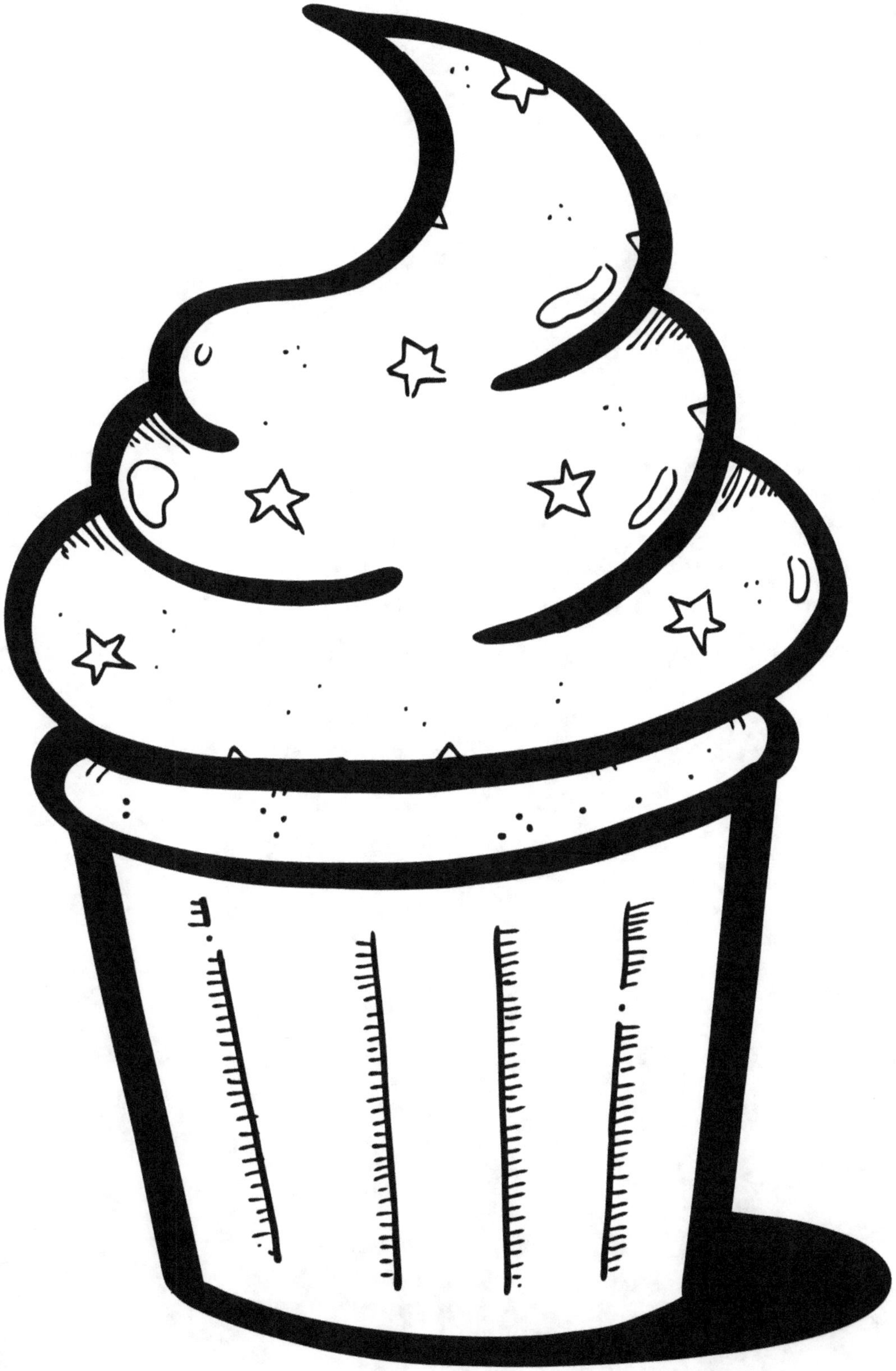

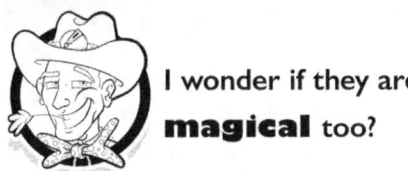 I wonder if they are **magical** too?

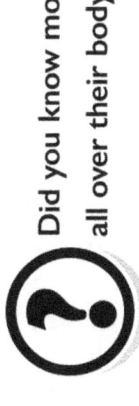

? Did you know most **Fish** have taste buds all over their body?

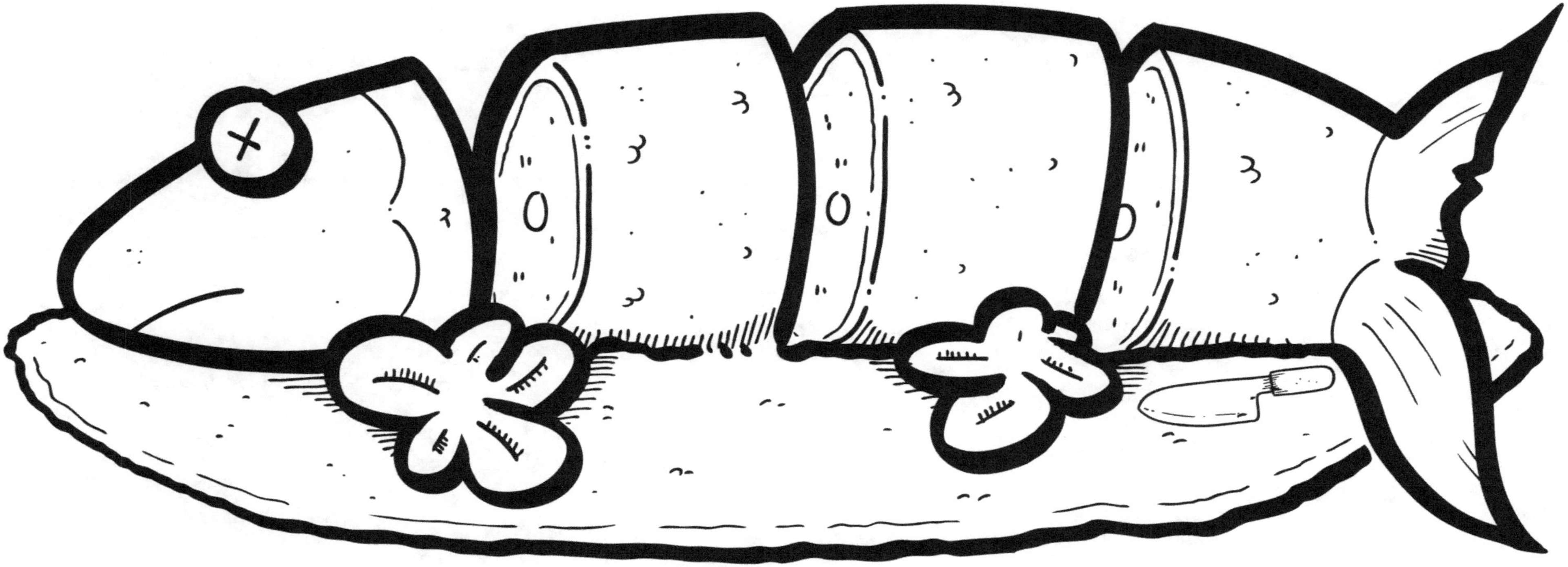

My favorite fish is **Swordfish!**

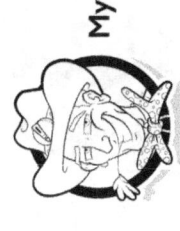

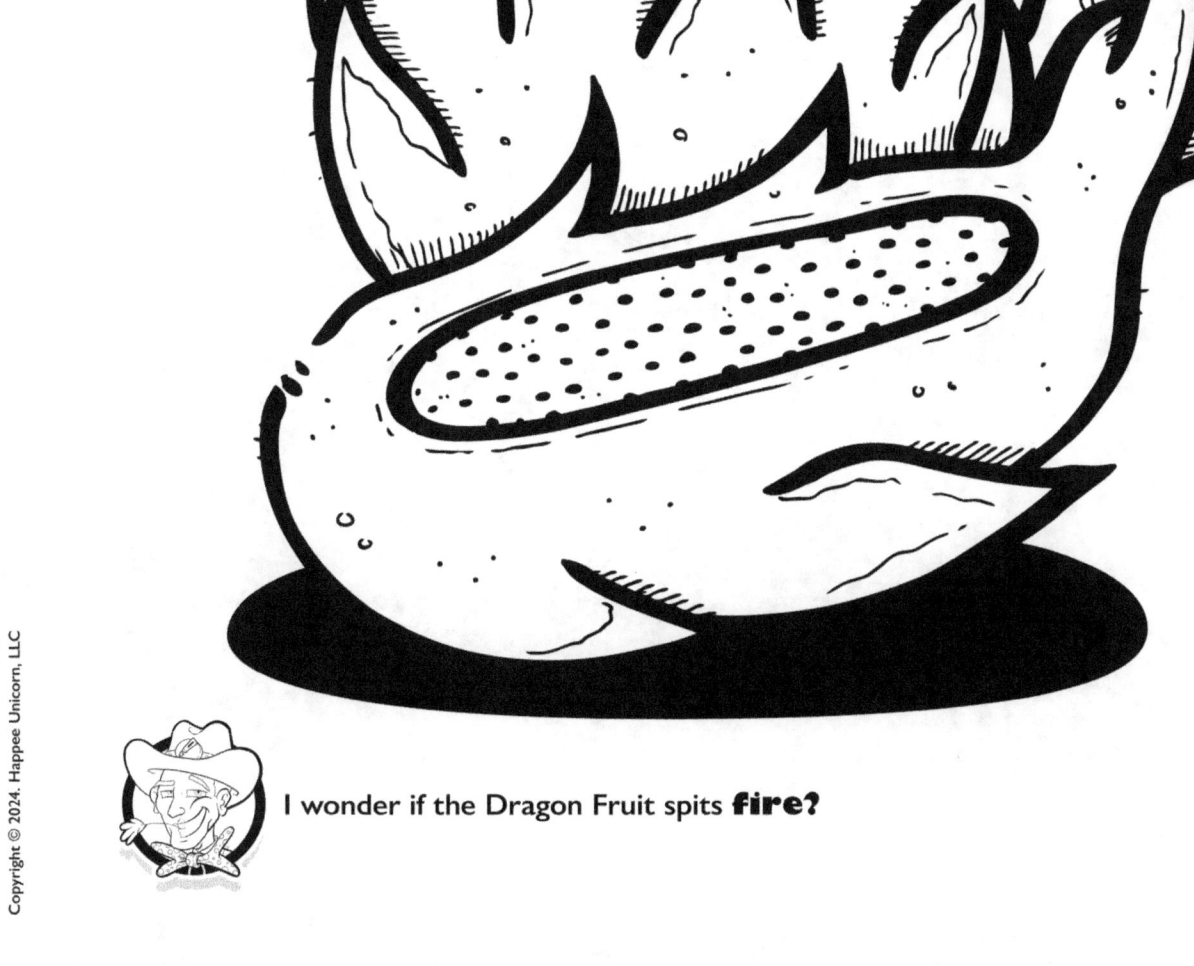

Did you know the **Dragon Fruit** blooms on a cactus for one night only? The cactus flower blooms in the evening and wilts the next day.

I wonder if the Dragon Fruit spits **fire?**

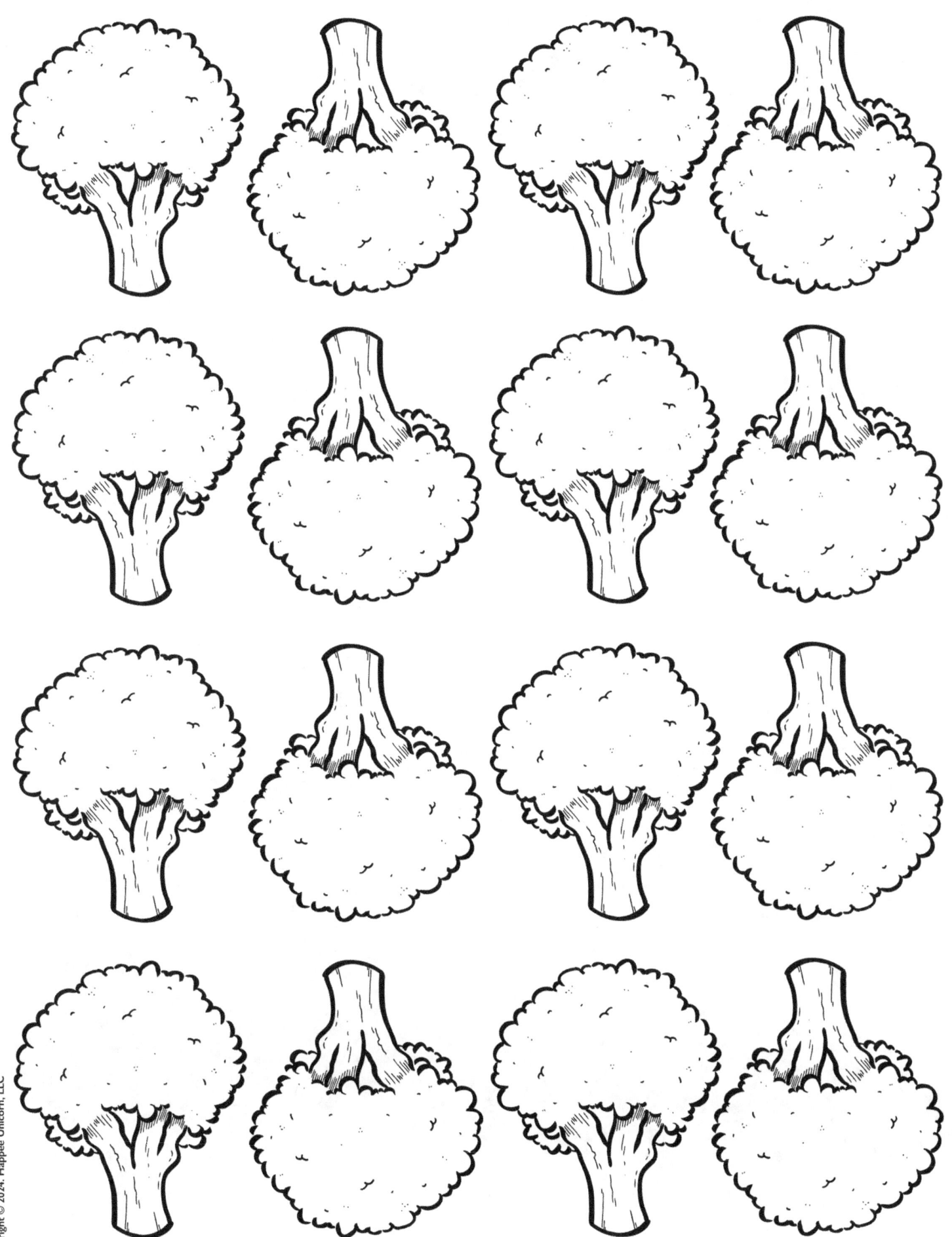

Did you know the first known **Pizzeria**, *Antica Pizzeria* in Naples, Italy, opened in 1738?

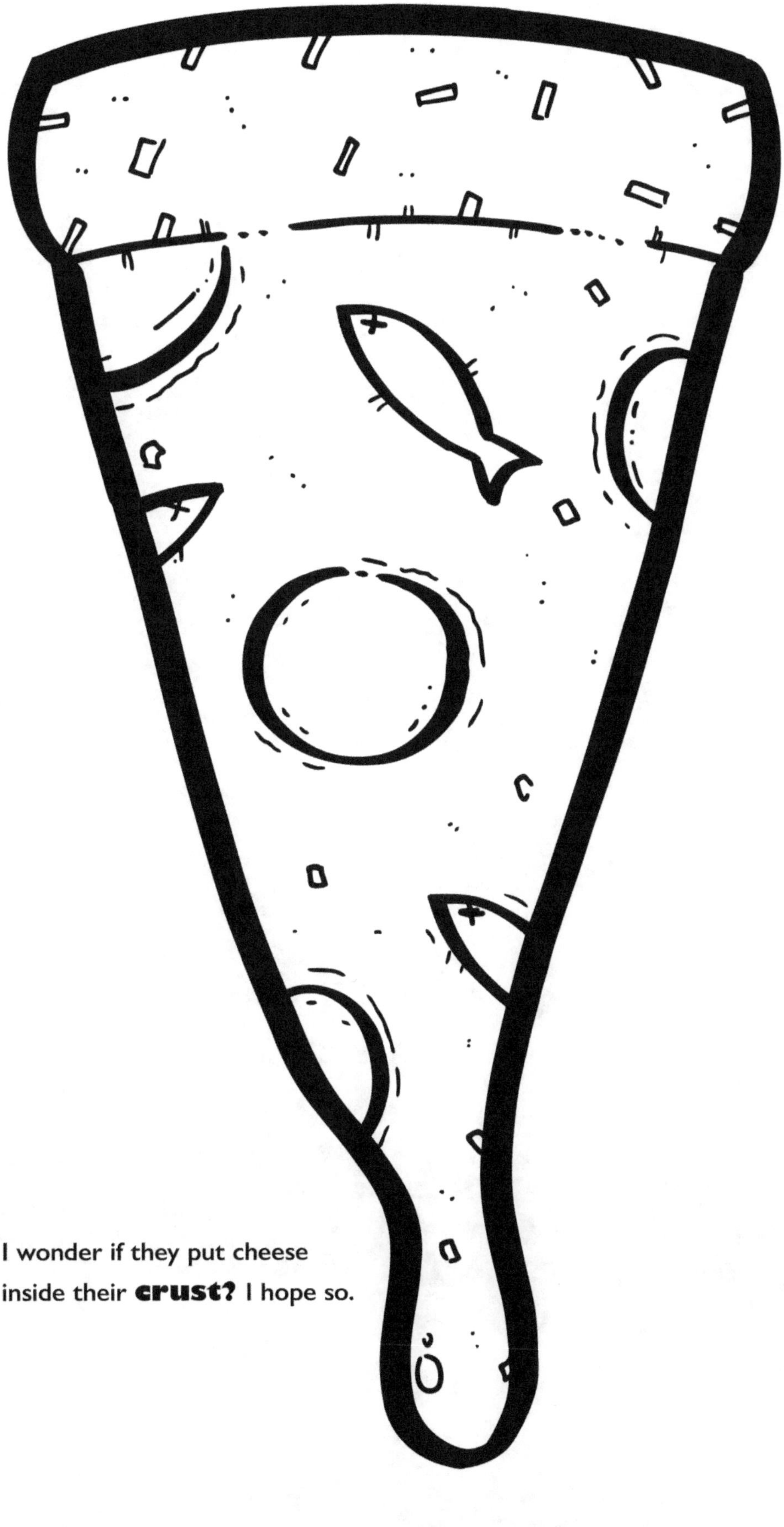

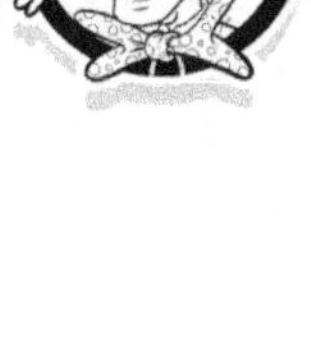

I wonder if they put cheese inside their **crust?** I hope so.

 Did you know January 27th is
National Chocolate Cake Day?

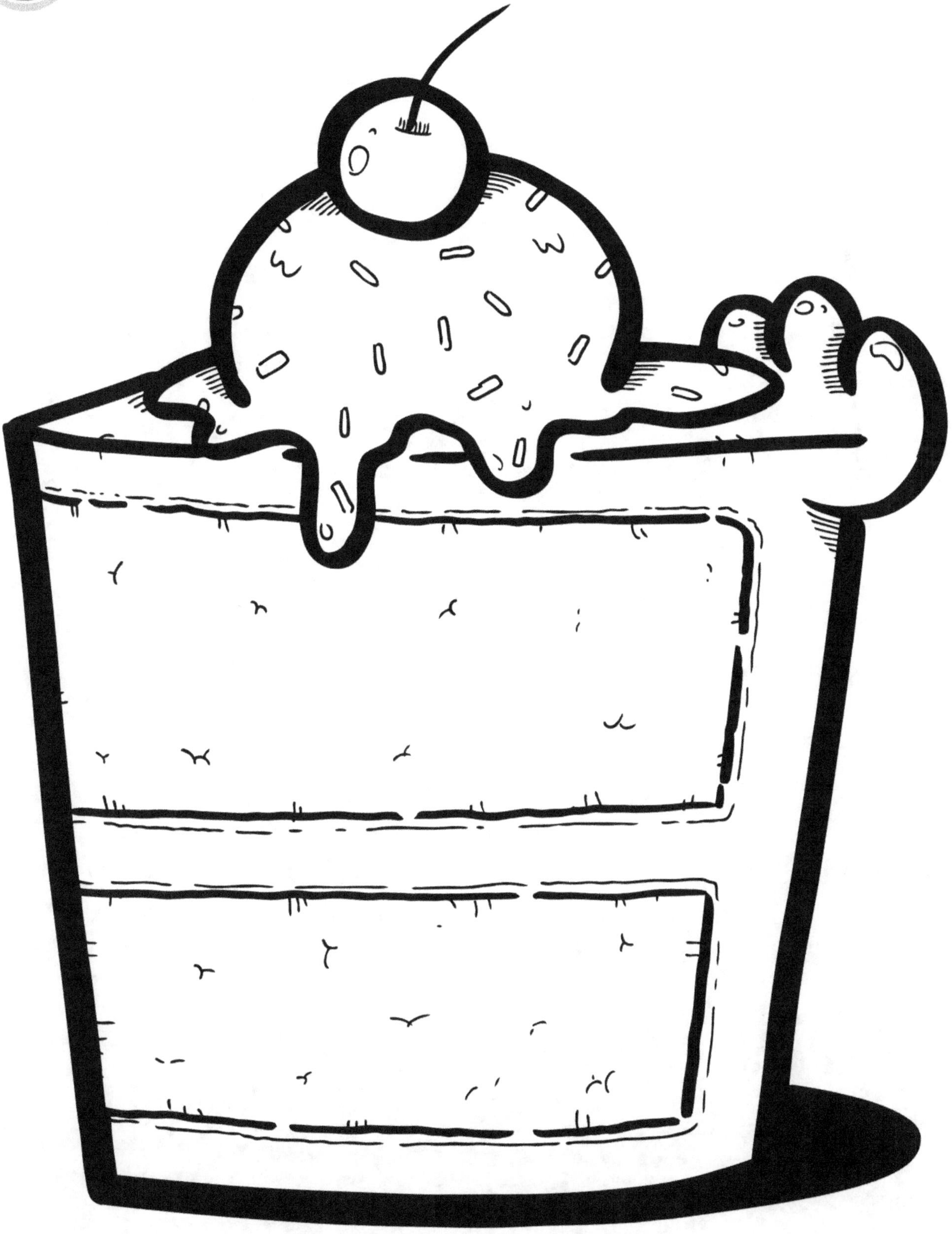

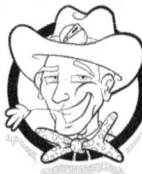 I'm going to eat an entire **cake** to myself. You know, to celebrate.

? Did you know **Spaghetti** is the plural form of the Italian word *Spaghetto?*

I like to put **pickle juice** in my spaghetti sauce. Try it. Trust me.

 Did you know Americans eat about 50 billion **Burgers** every year? That's like every person eating 3 burgers a week.

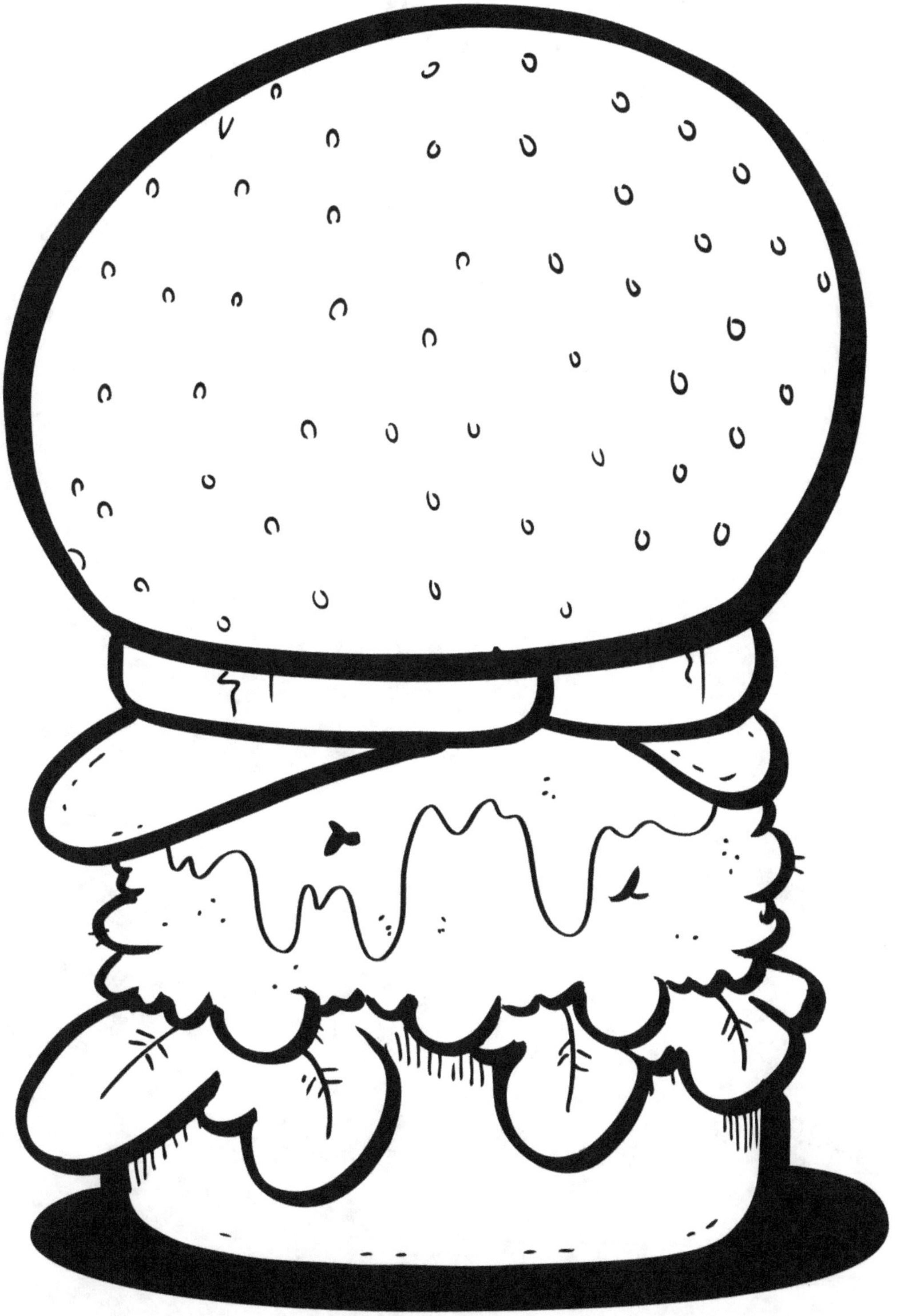

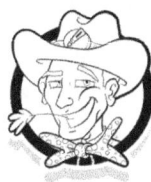 Don't worry, I'll start **eating** more burgers to bring that weekly number down.

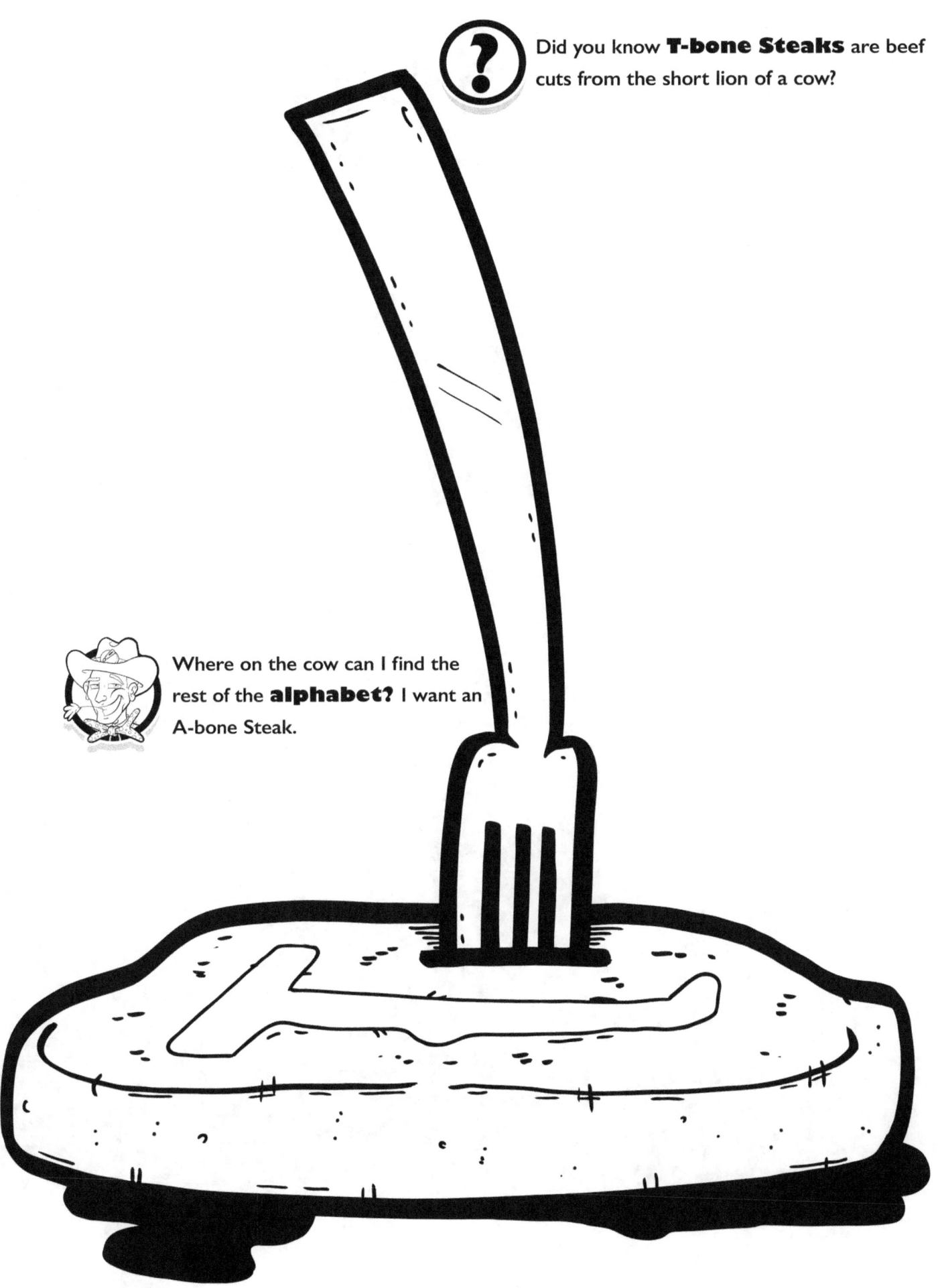

I like to call them **Flippity Floppity Flappy Jacks!**

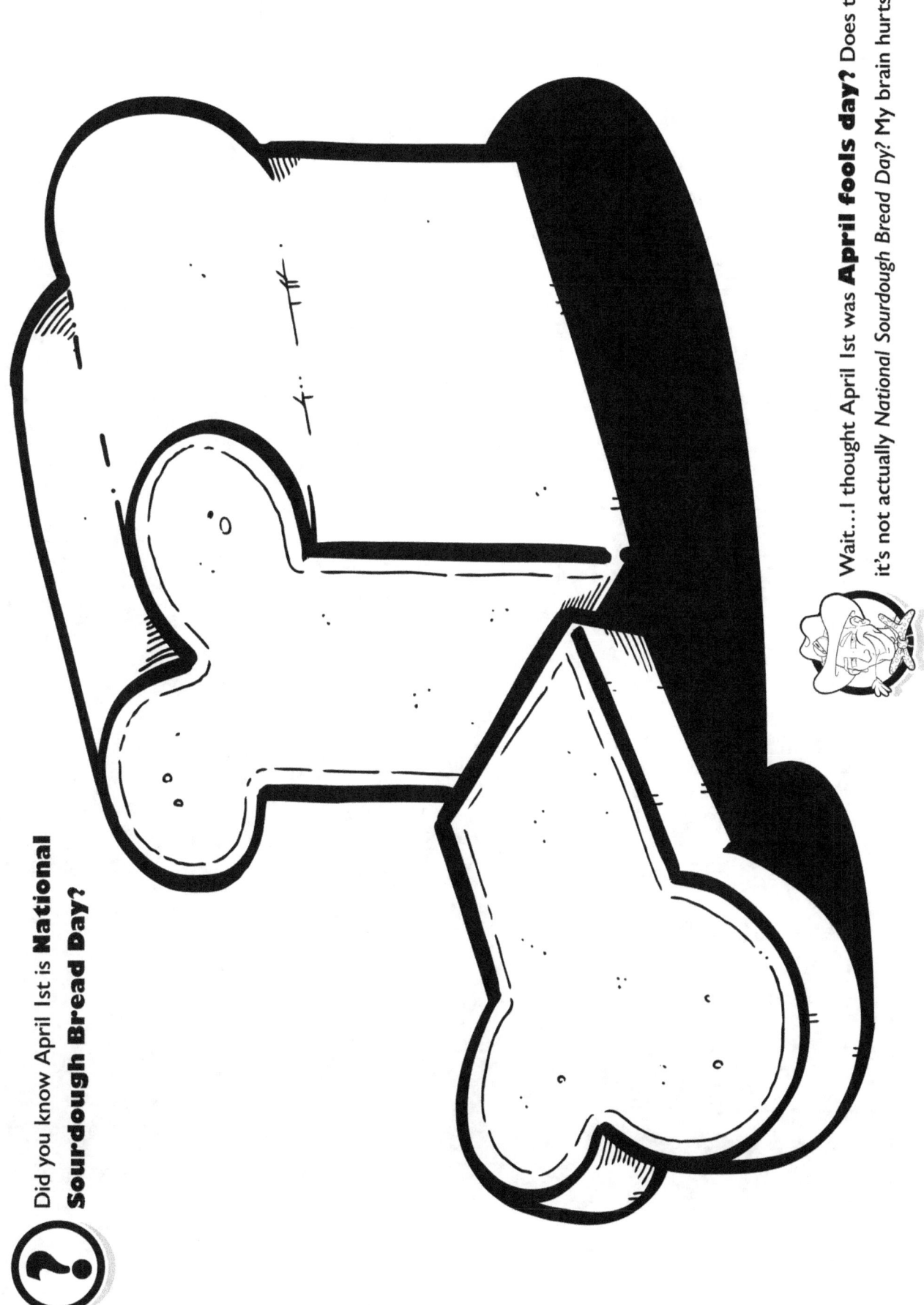

Did you know April 1st is **National Sourdough Bread Day?**

Wait…I thought April 1st was **April fools day?** Does that mean it's not actually *National Sourdough Bread Day?* My brain hurts.

? Did you know a **Lobster** egg is referred to as a roe?

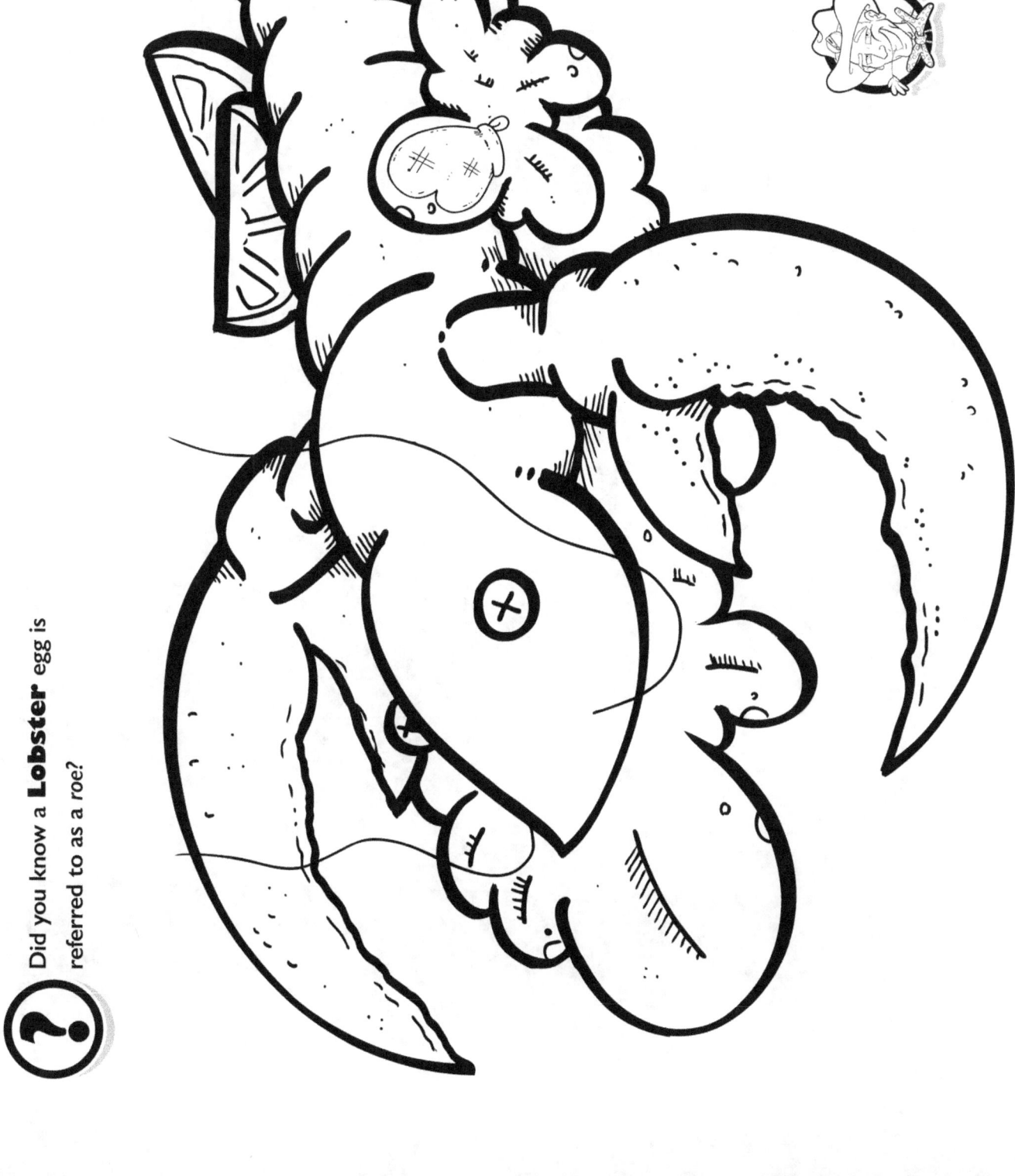

Can I **paint** them for Easter?

? Did you know that **lettuce** is a member of the sunflower family?

Mmmmm...I'll take my **sunflower salad** to go please.

Did you know, according to the *Oxford English Dictionary*, the word hamburgers was first abbreviated to **'Burger'** in 1939?

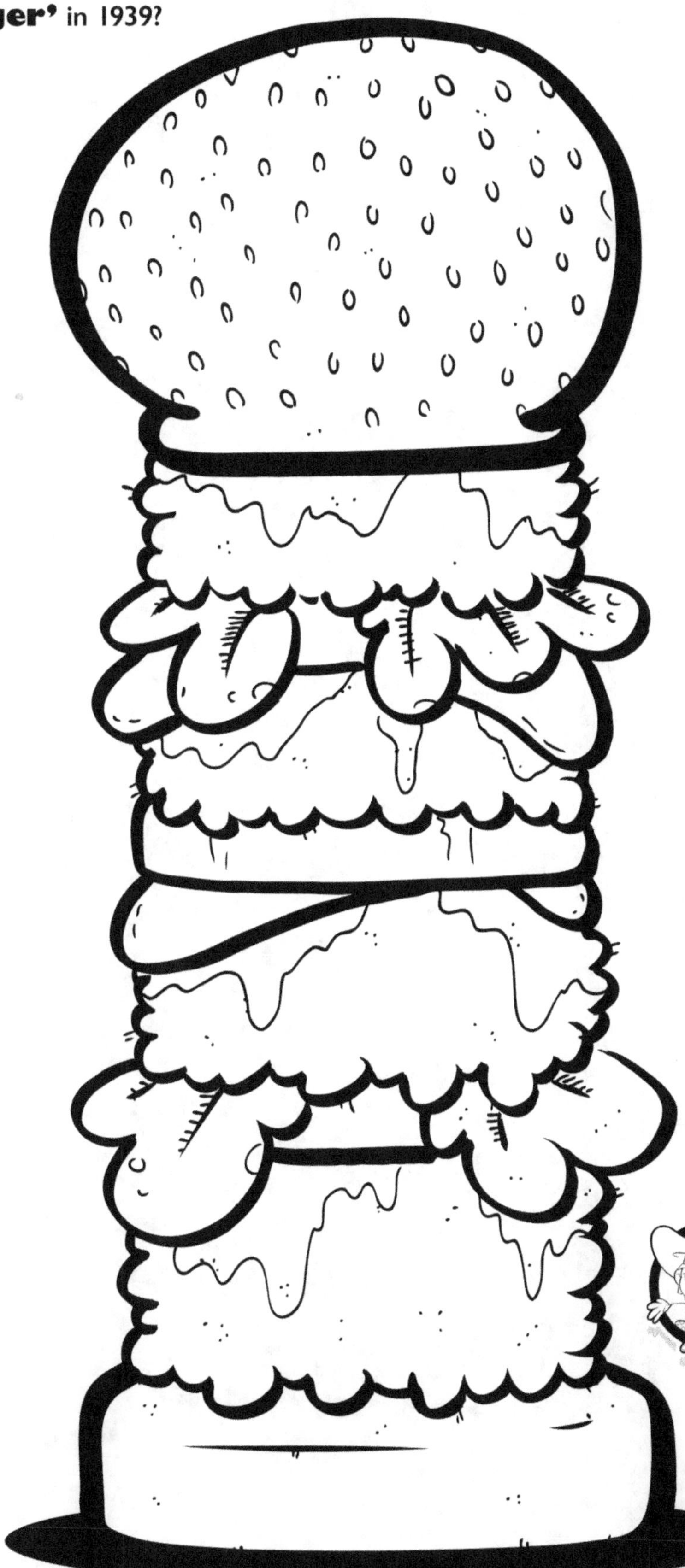

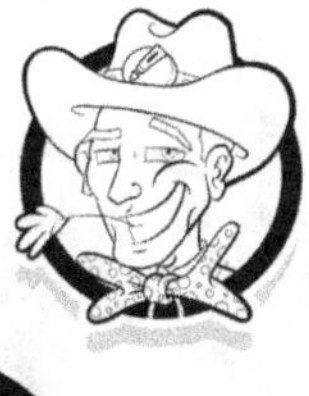

Do you think you could **eat** this mega burger stack?

? Did you know the dish used to serve a **Banana Split** is called a 'boat?'

I'd **sail** across the world in a Banana Split boat!

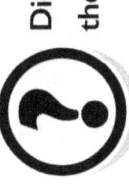 Did you know the word **Sushi** actually refers to the seasoned rice and not the fish?

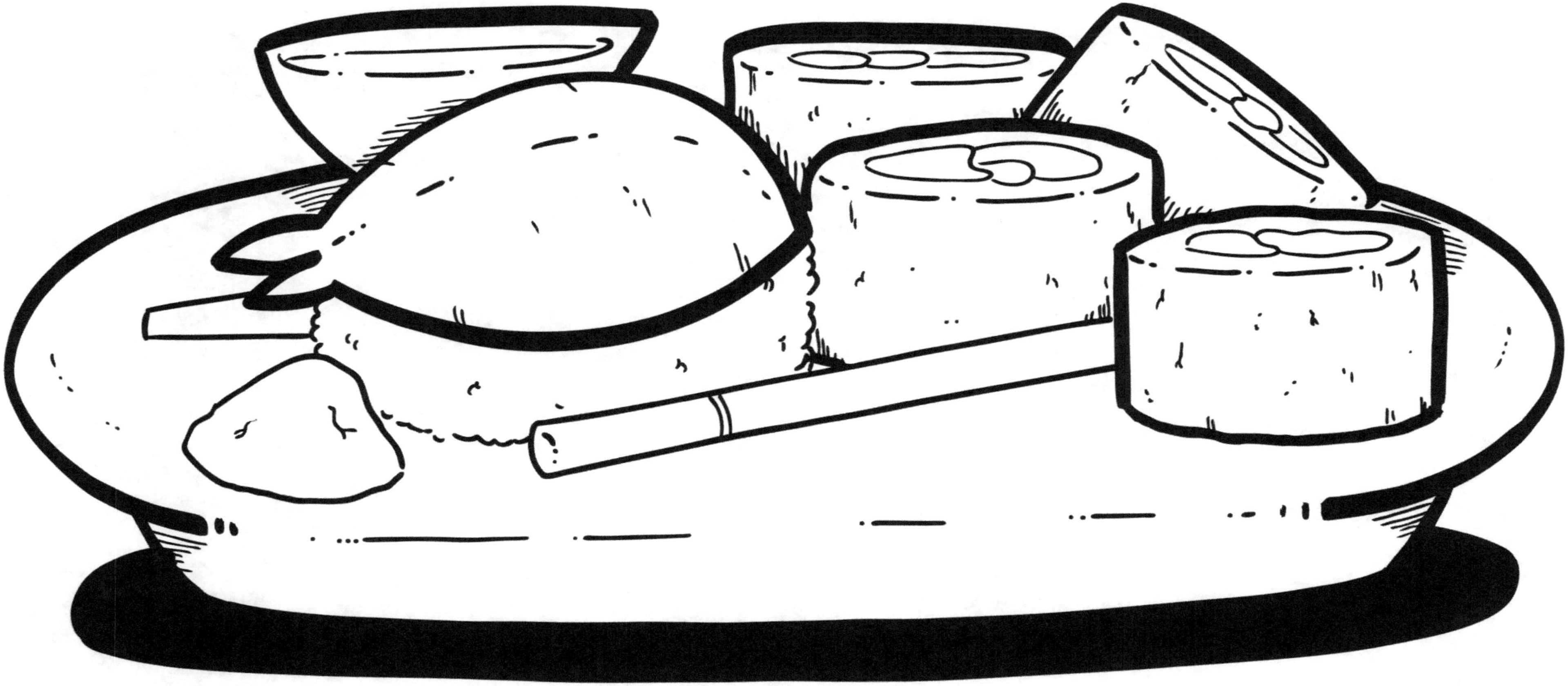

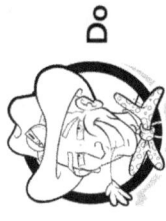 Do you **like** Sushi?

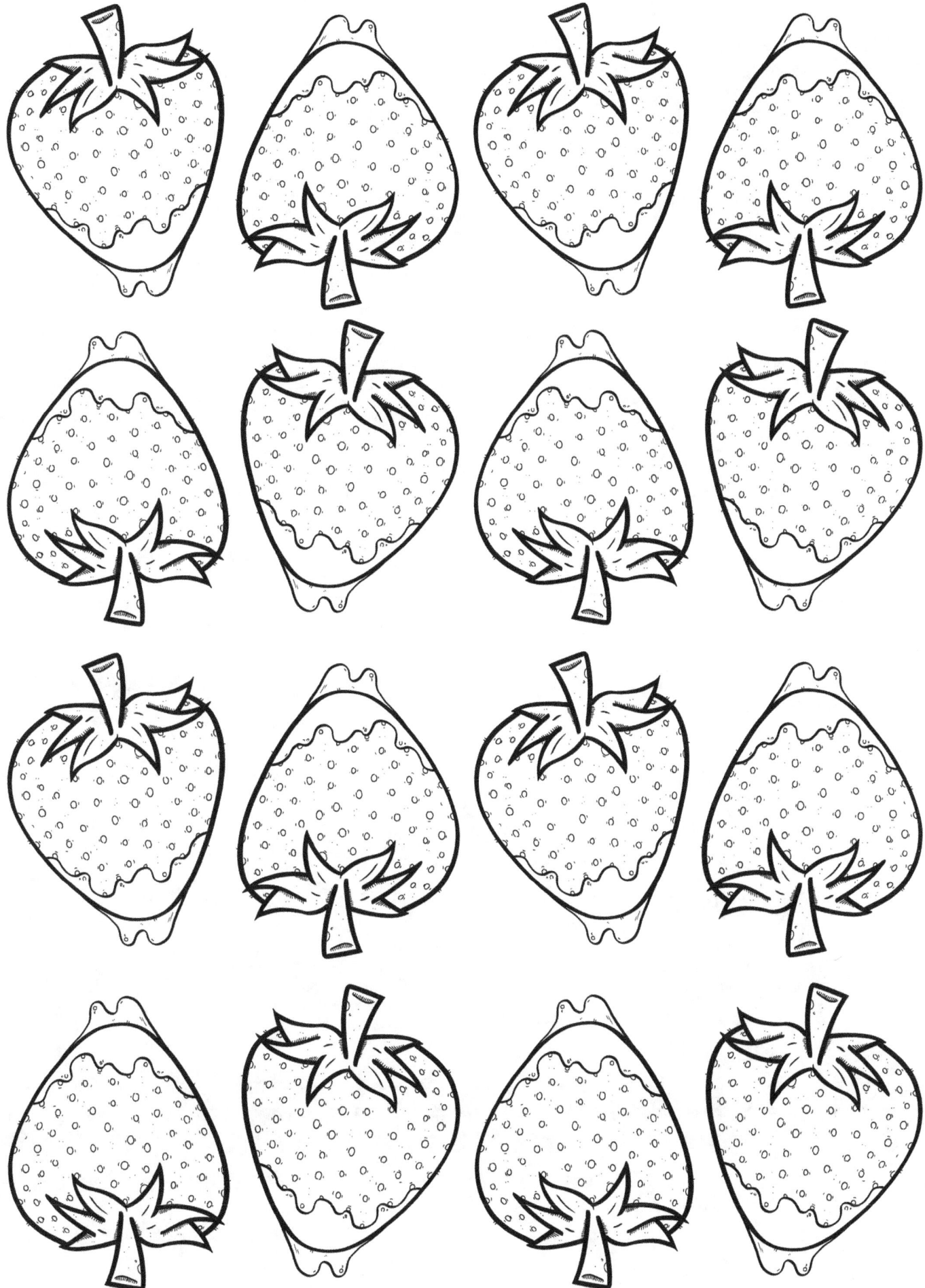

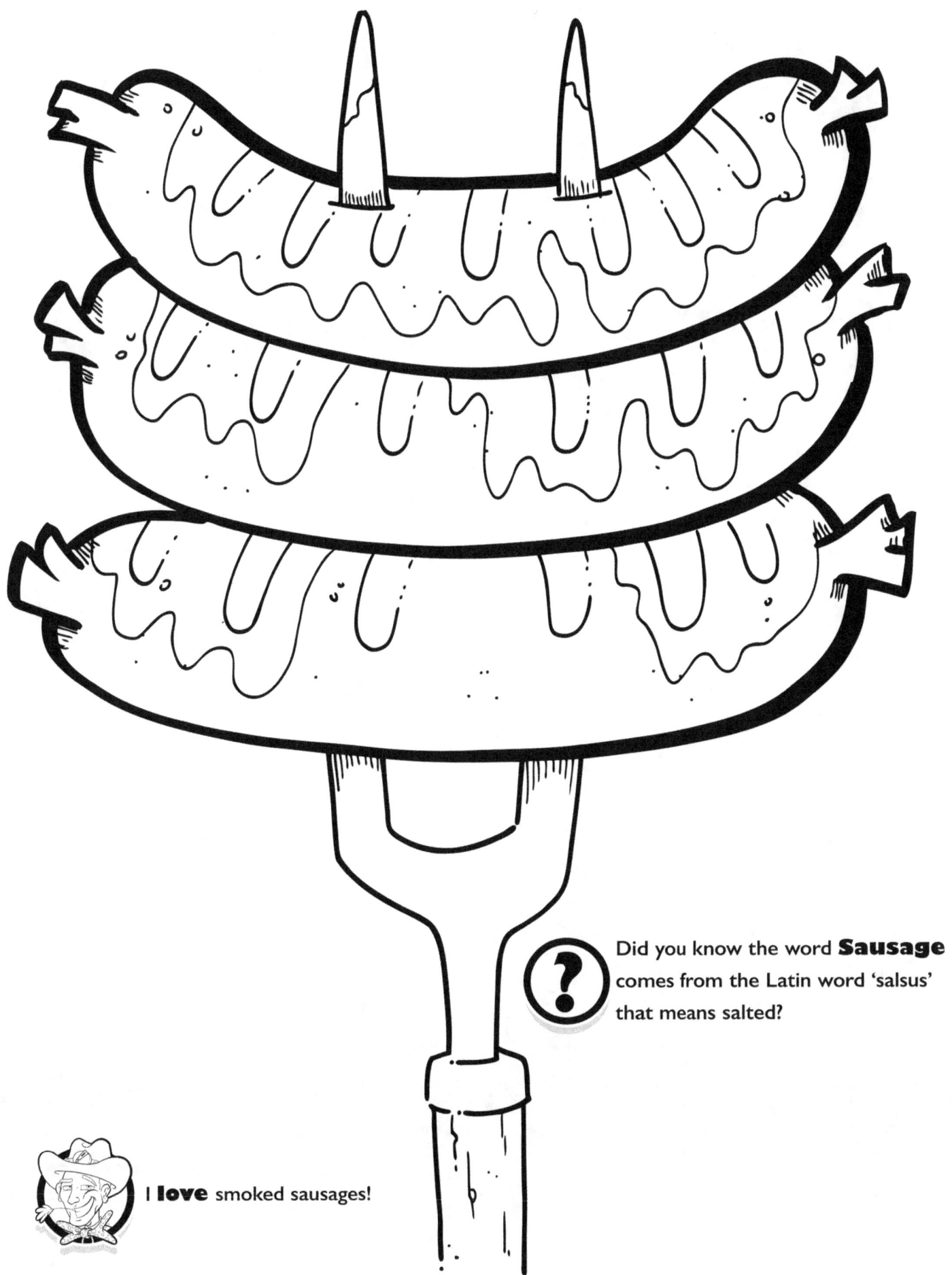

Did you know the word **Sausage** comes from the Latin word 'salsus' that means salted?

I **love** smoked sausages!

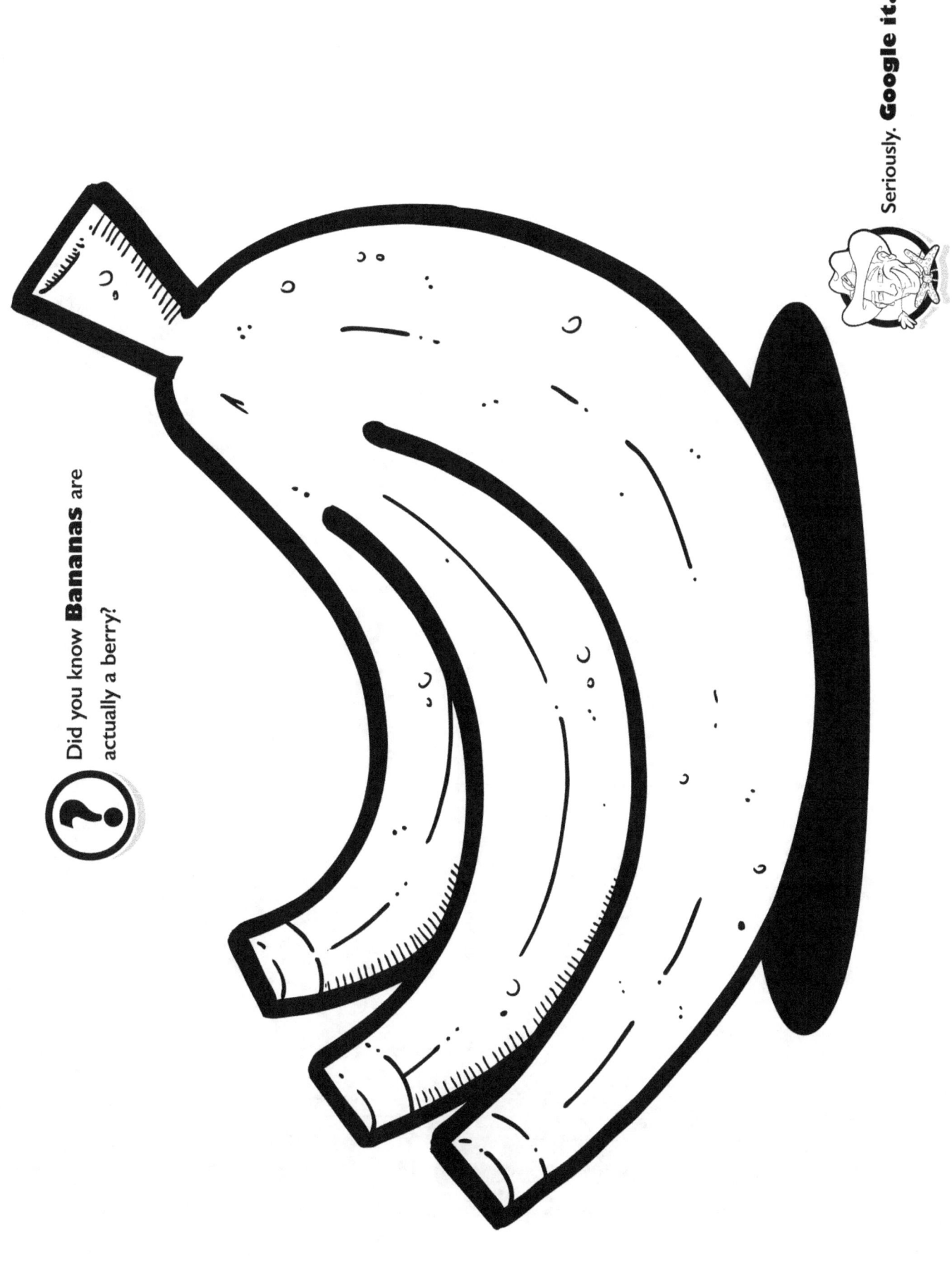

Did you know **Bananas** are actually a berry?

Seriously. **Google it.**

Did you know the tallest stack of **Donuts** stood over 43 inches tall?

I tried to beat that record, then I **ate** all my donuts.

? Did you know **National Taco Day** is October 4th?

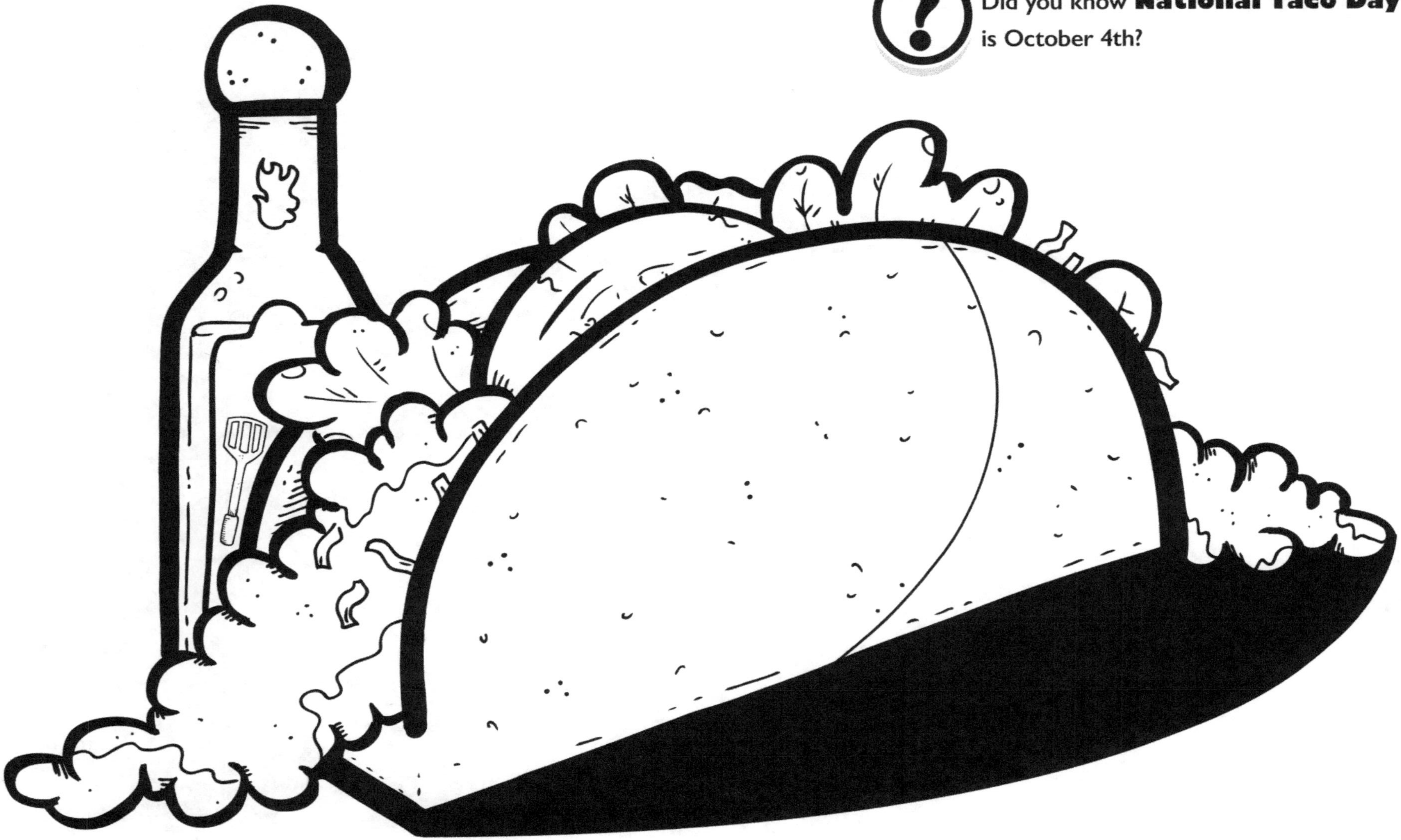

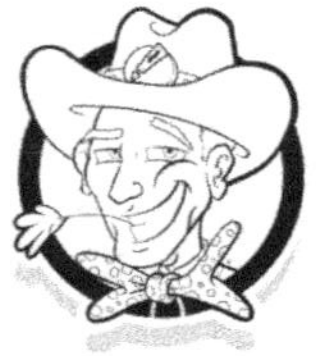

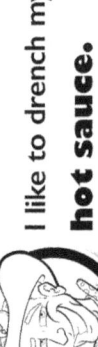

I like to drench my tacos in **hot sauce.**

? Did you know there are over 10,000 different species of **Mold?**

Gross!

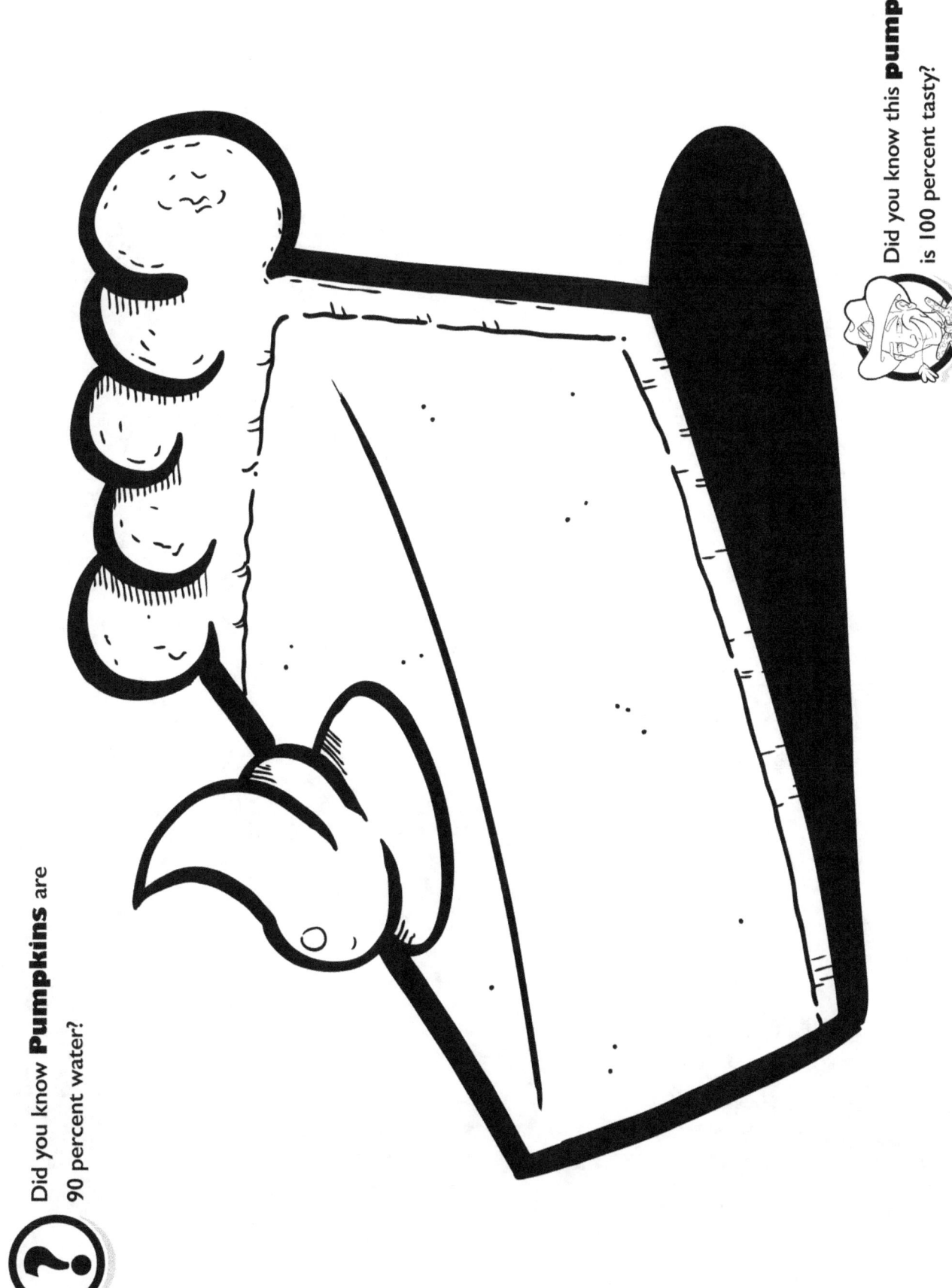

Did you know **Pumpkins** are 90 percent water?

Did you know this **pumpkin pie** is 100 percent tasty?

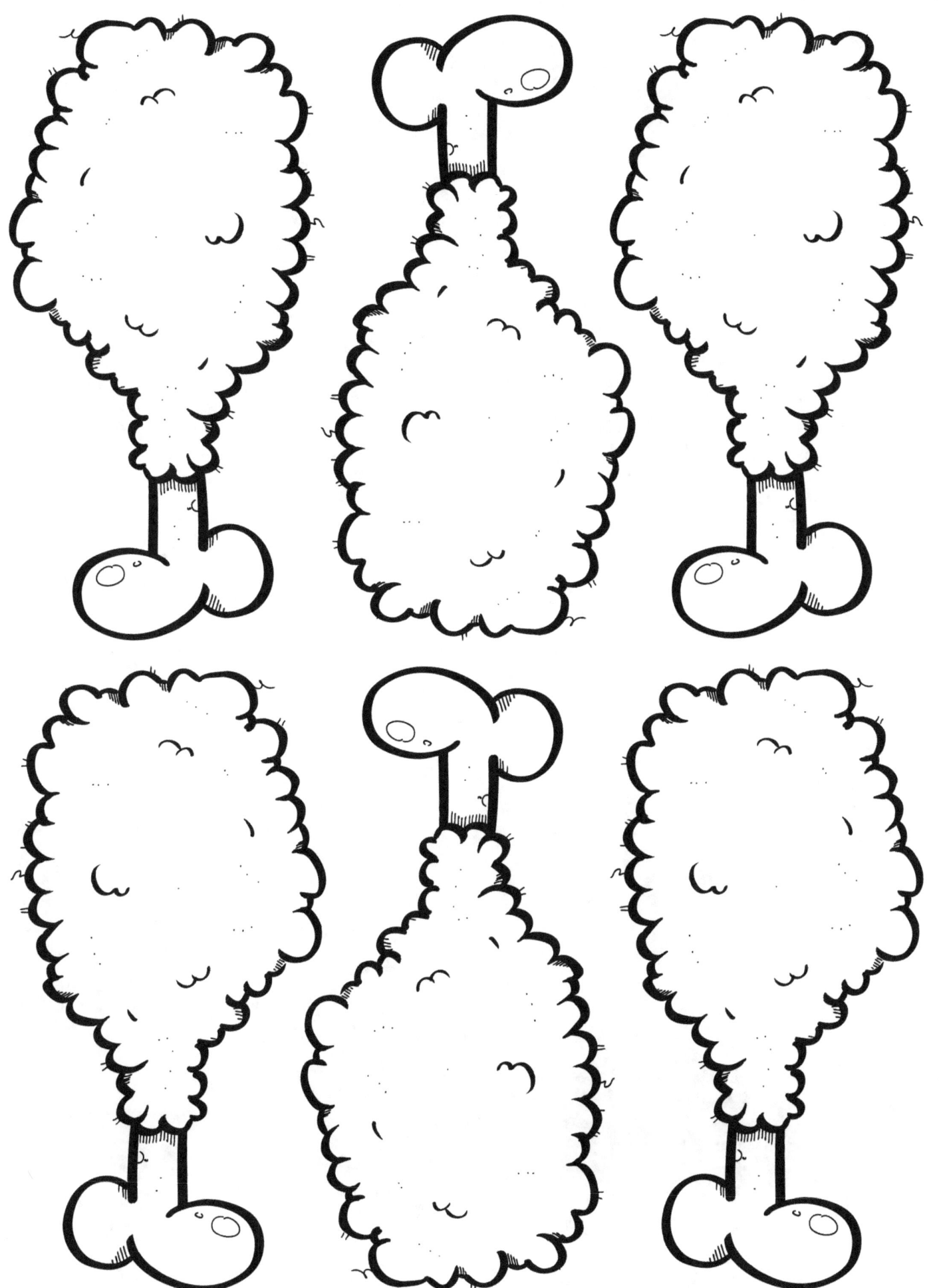

? Did you know it takes about 400 cocoa beans to make a single pound of **Chocolate?**

How many **cocoa beans** to fill my swimming pool?

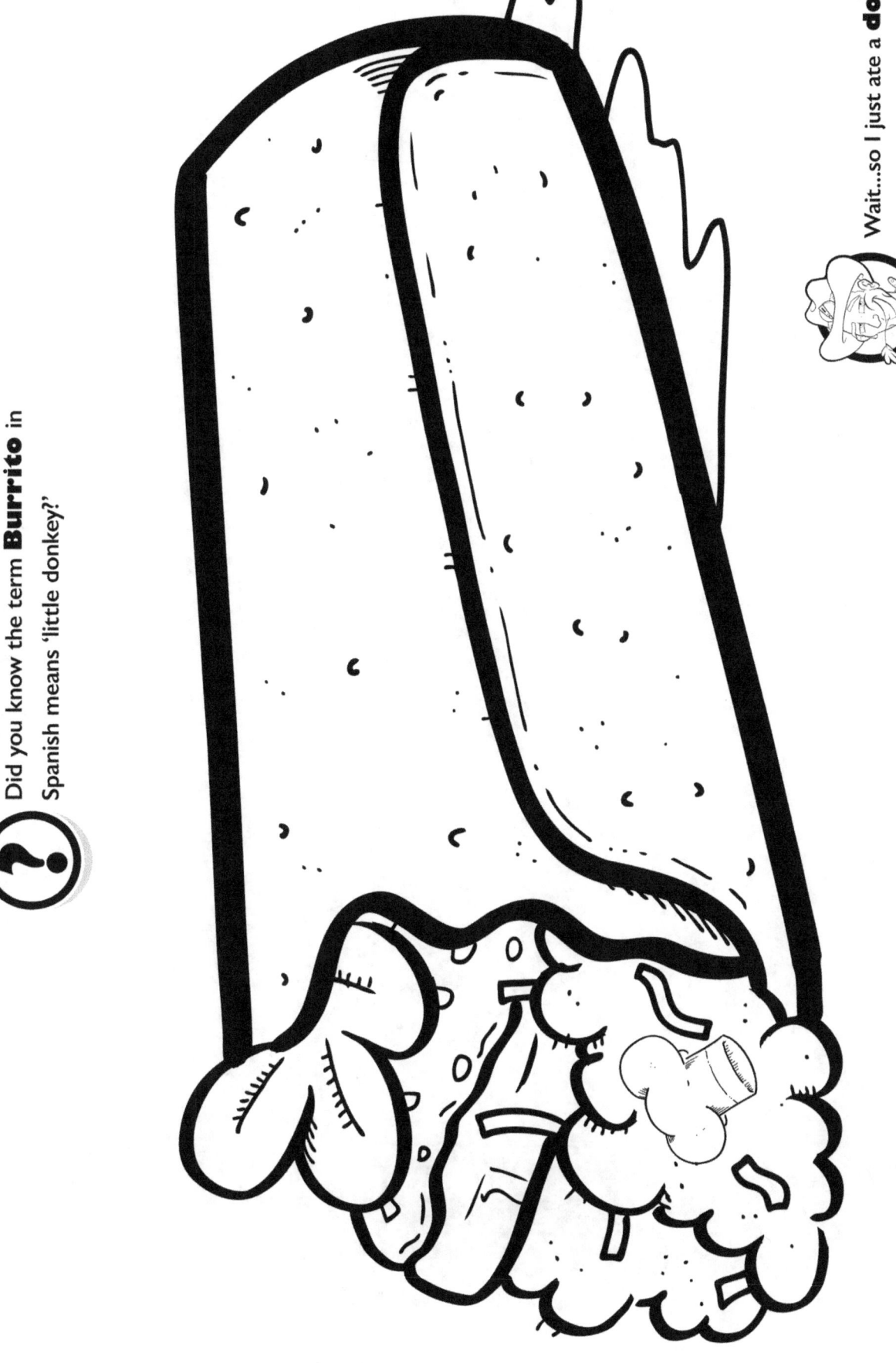

? Did you know the term **Burrito** in Spanish means 'little donkey?'

Wait...so I just ate a **donkey?**

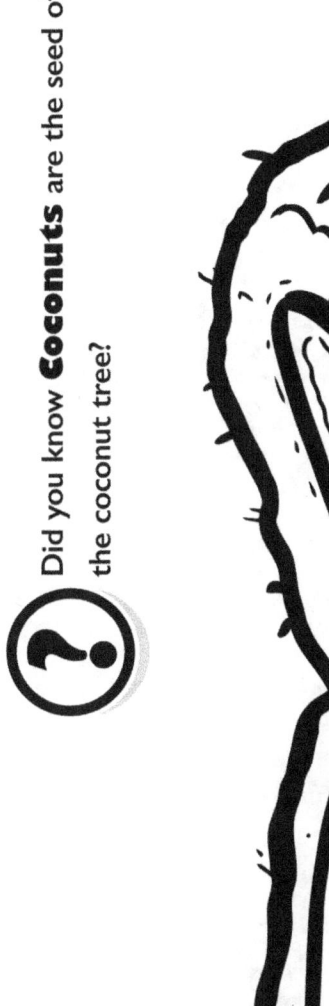

? Did you know **Coconuts** are the seed of the coconut tree?

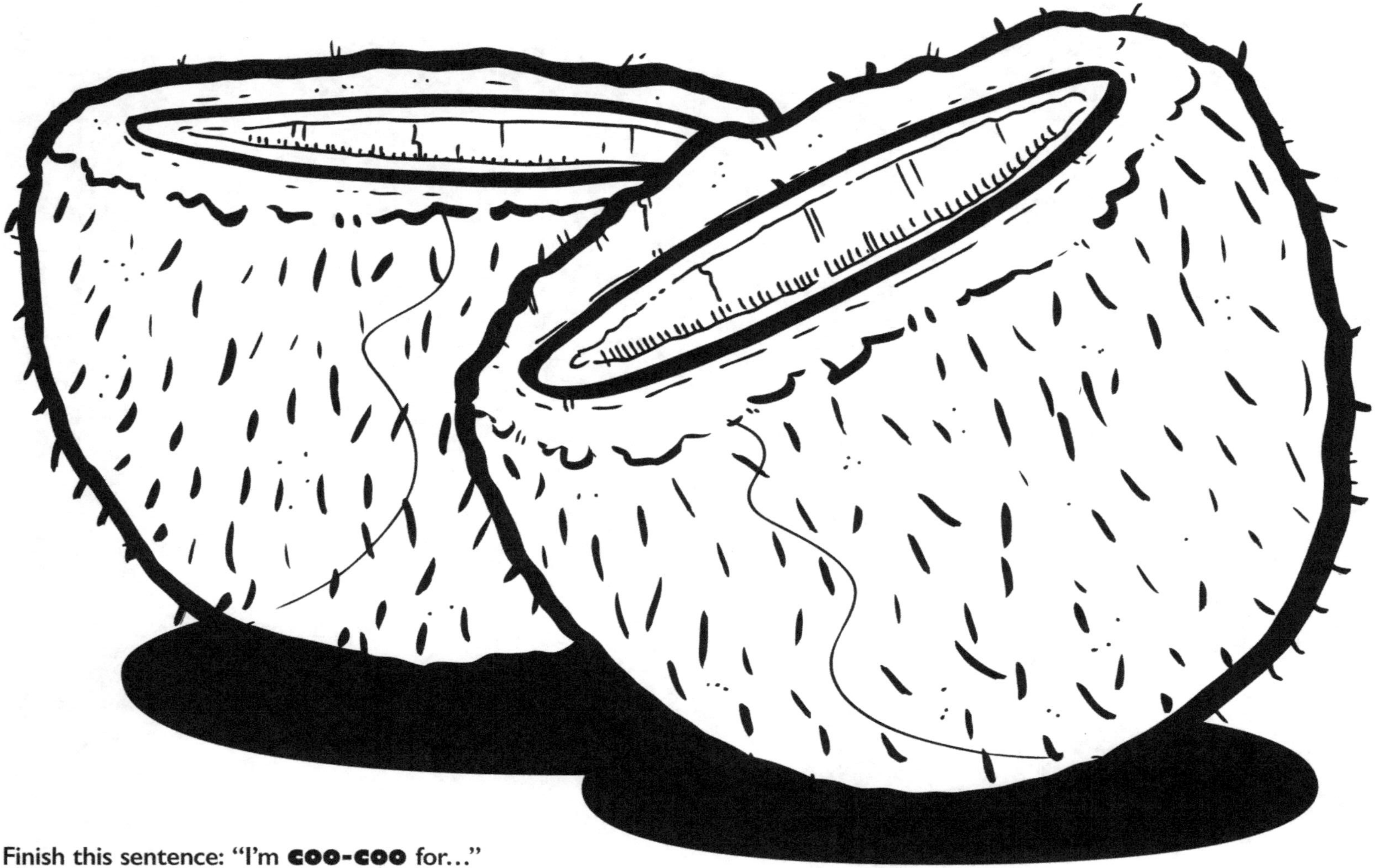

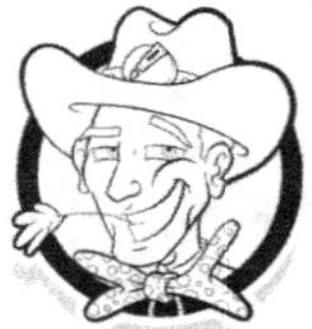

Finish this sentence: "I'm **COO-COO** for…"

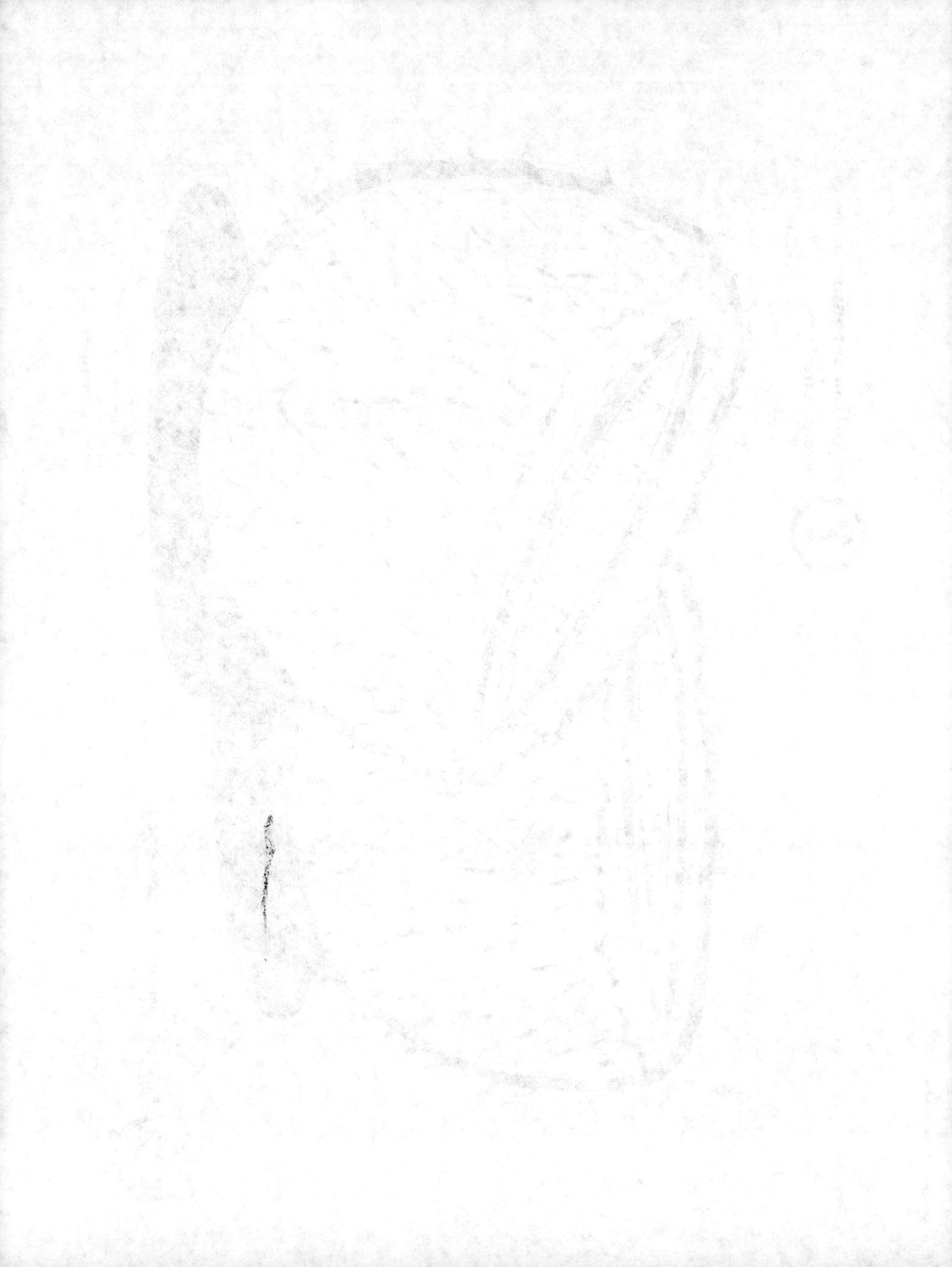

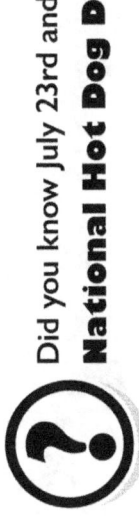

Did you know July 23rd and September 10th are
National Hot Dog Days?

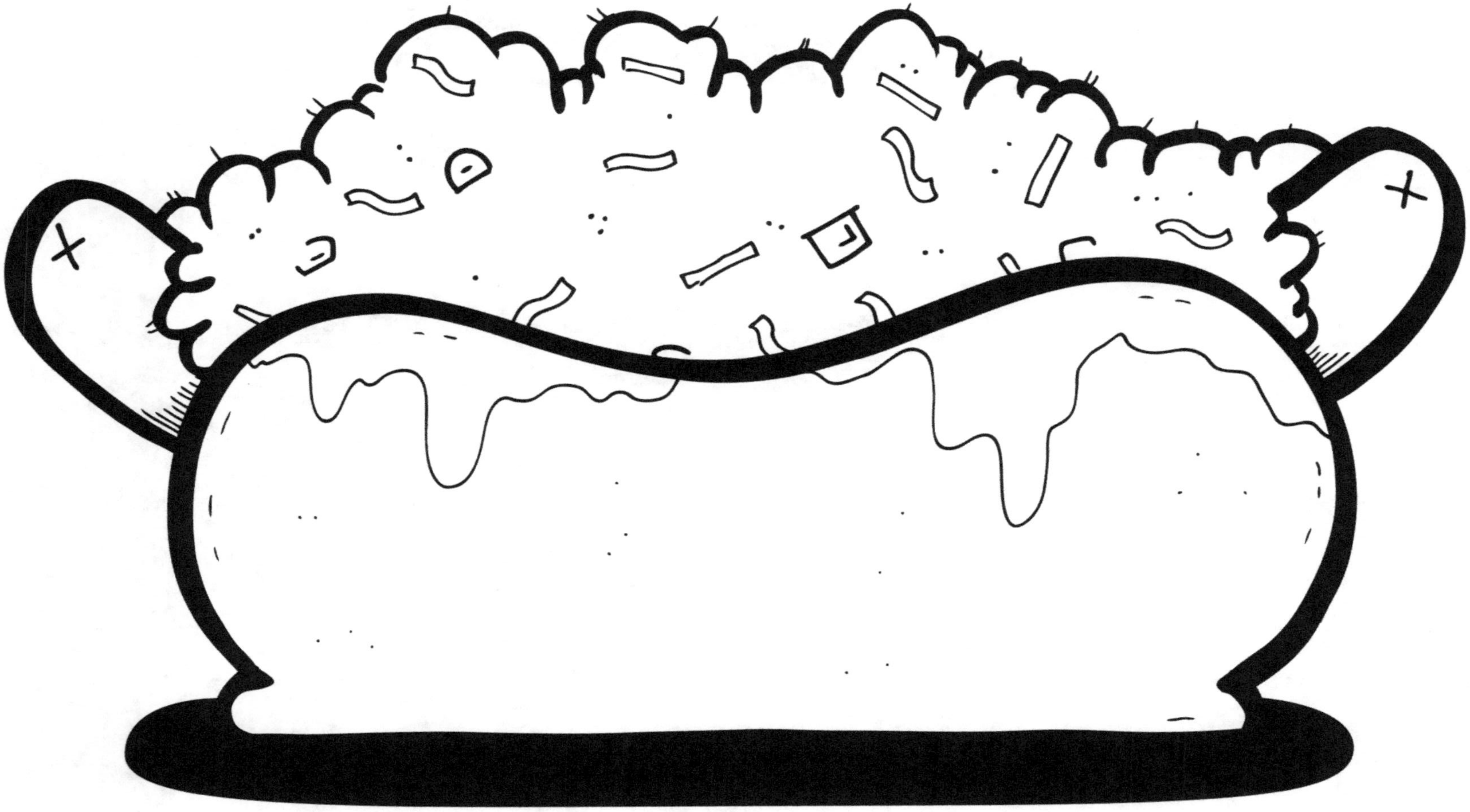

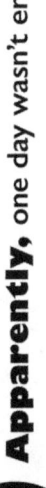

Apparently, one day wasn't enough.

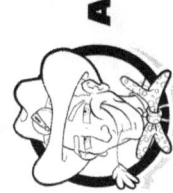

? Did you know the *Texas State Fair* sells over 630,000 **Corn Dogs** every year?

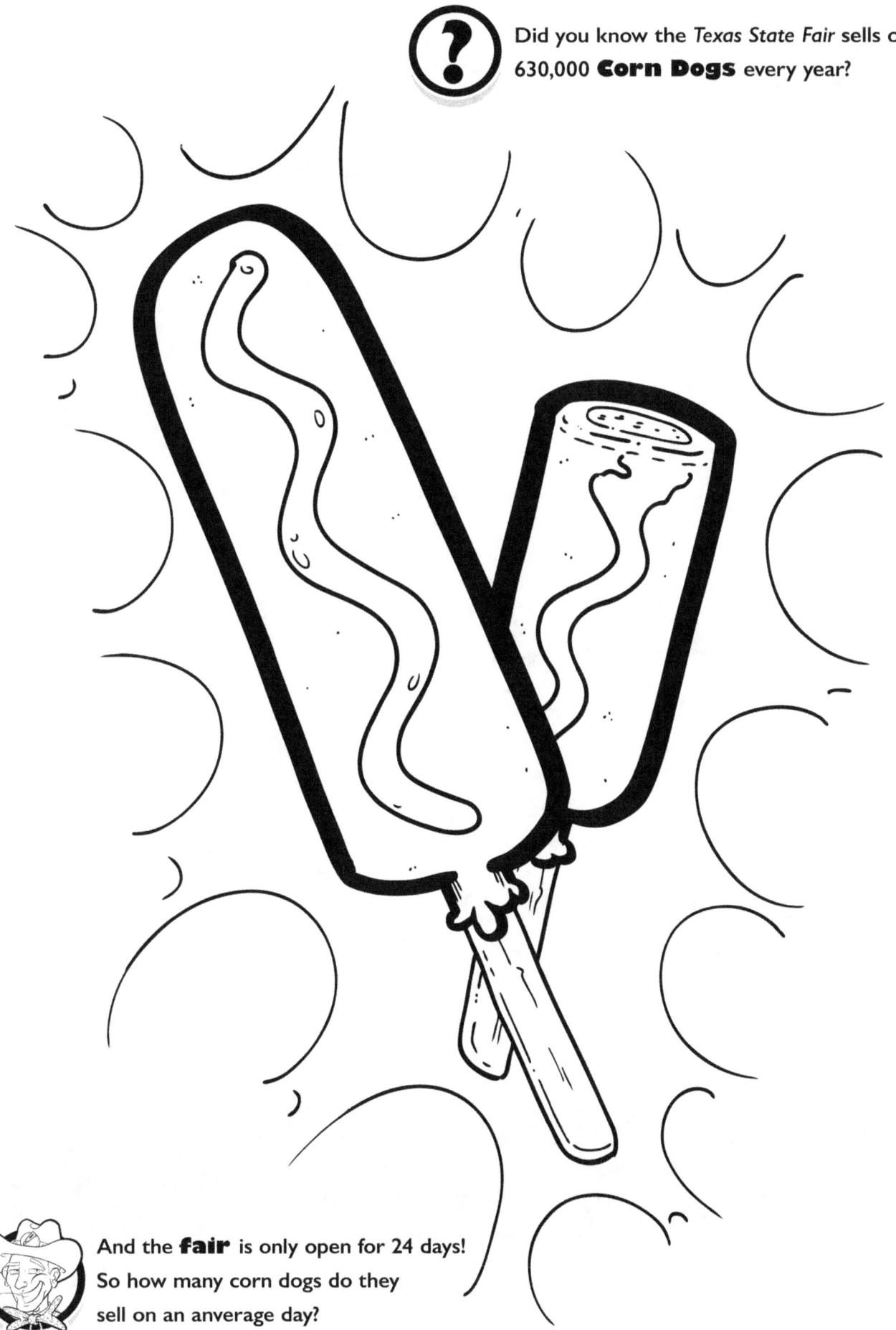

And the **fair** is only open for 24 days! So how many corn dogs do they sell on an anverage day?

Did you know Doctor John T. Dorrance, a chemist with the Campbell Company, invented **Condensed Soup** in 1897?

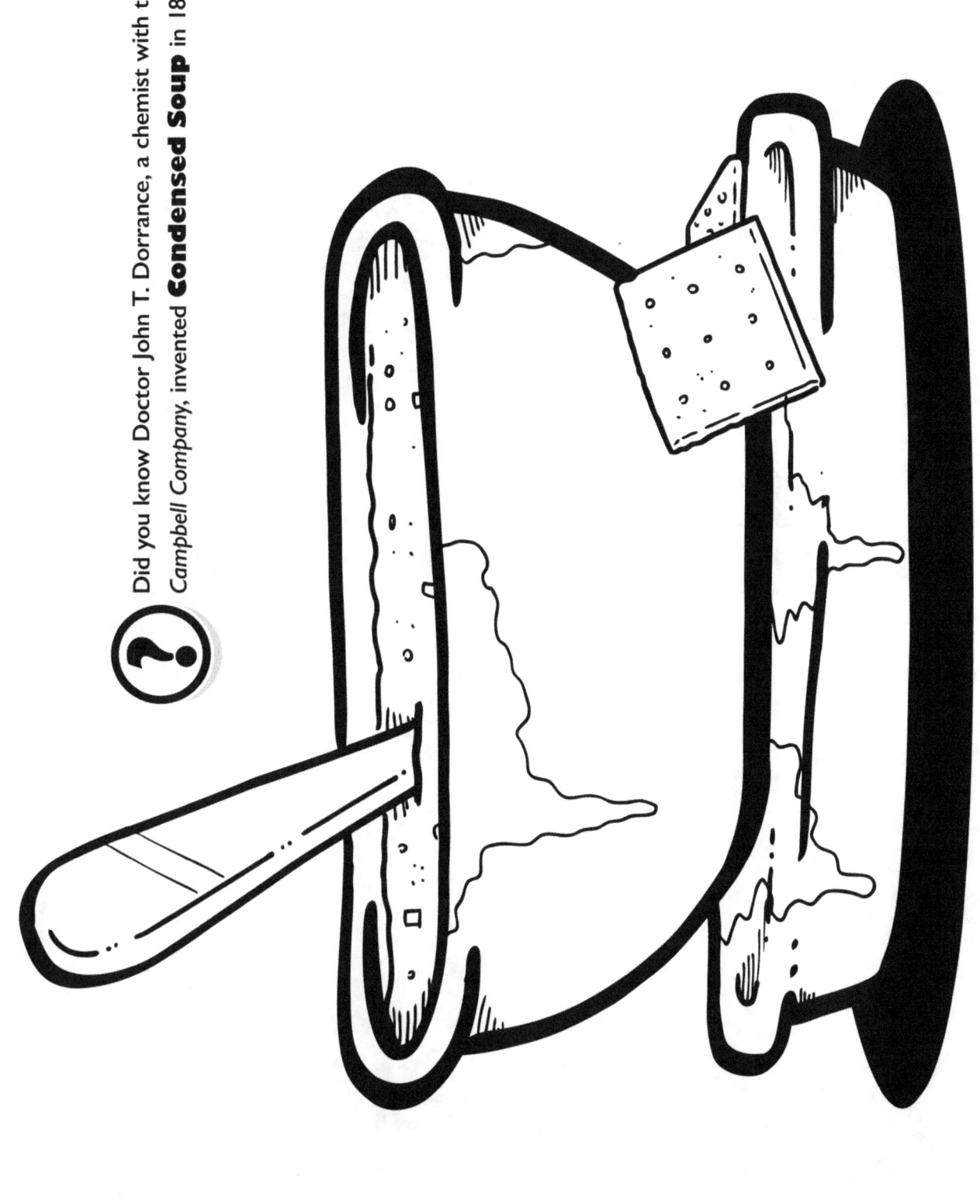

Cabbage Soup is my favorite!

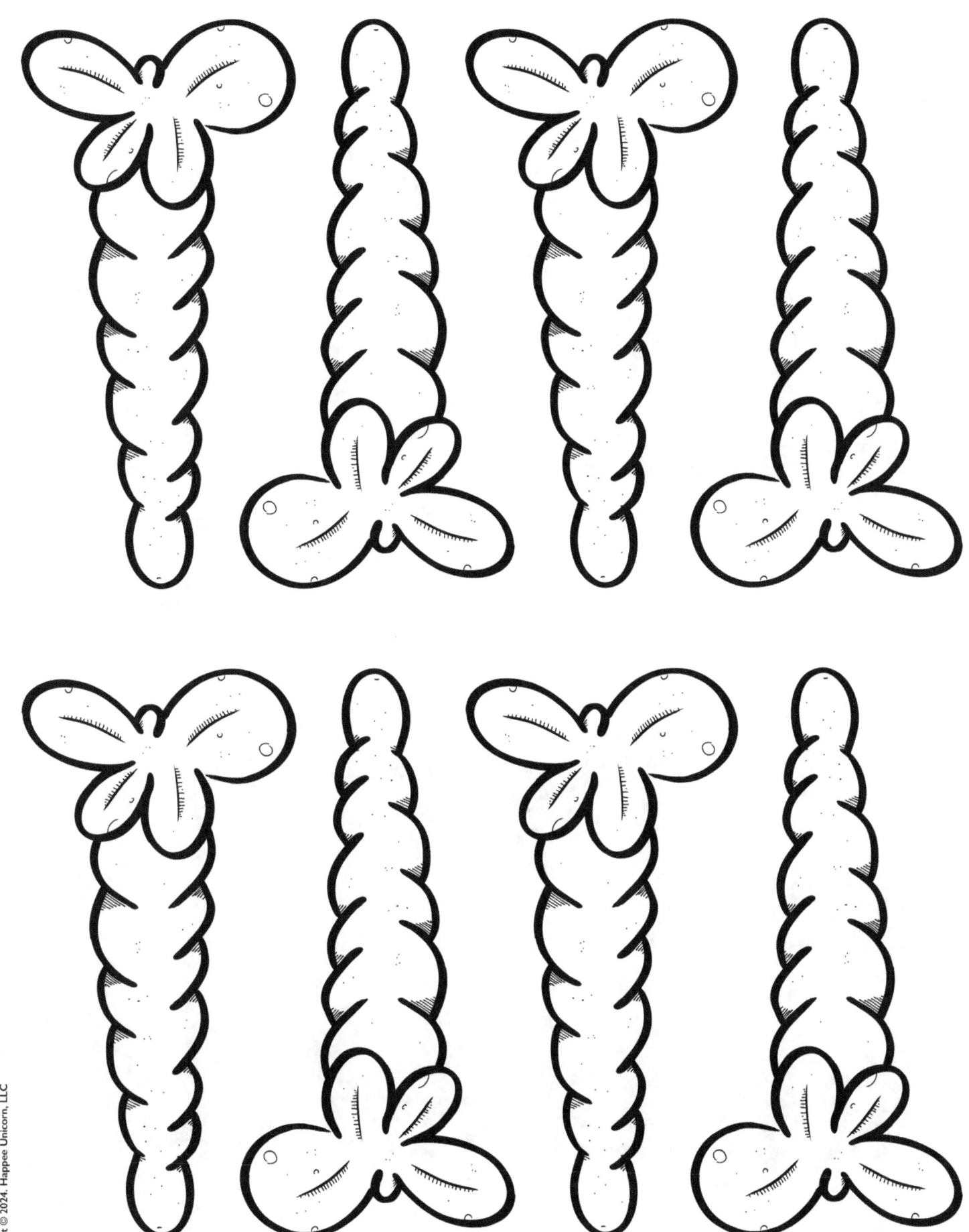

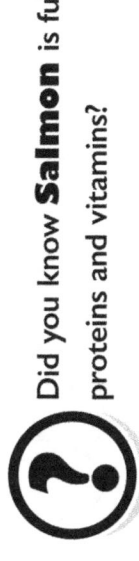

Did you know **Salmon** is full of proteins and vitamins?

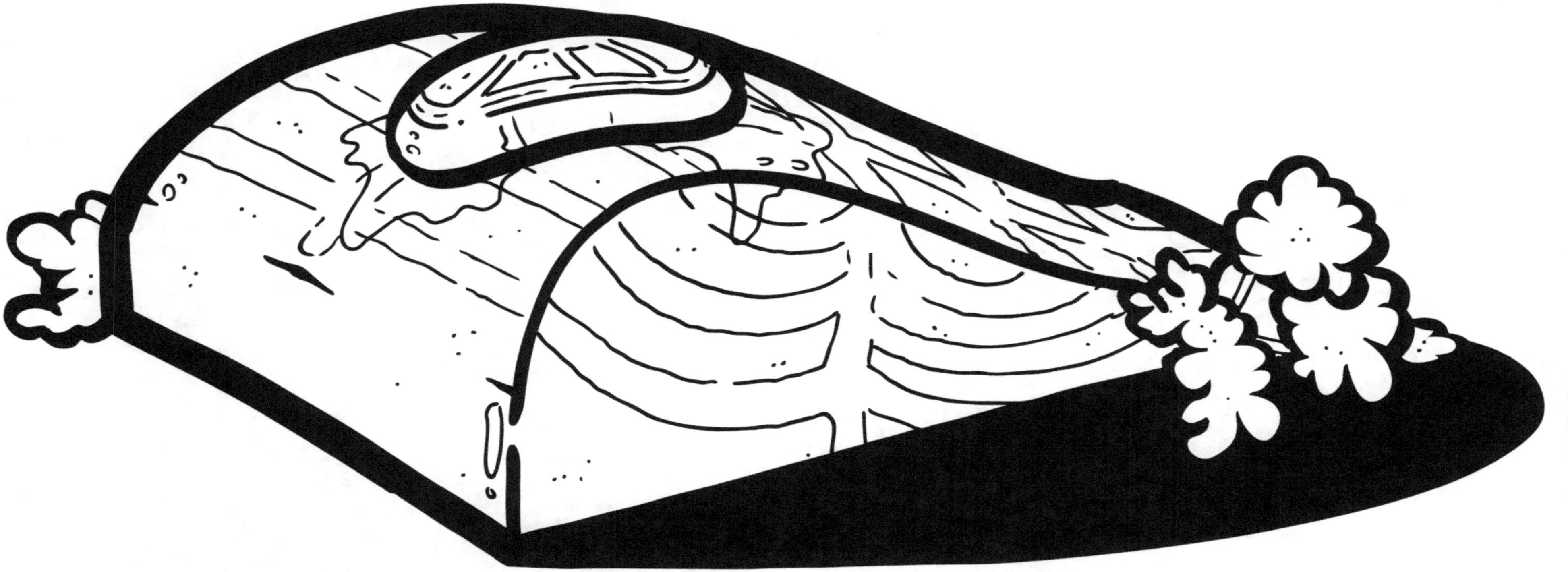

Mmmm...good and *good for you!*

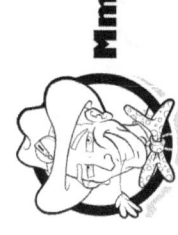

? Did you know an estimated 46 million **Turkeys** are consumed on Thanksgiving alone?

Lets start **Operation Save The Turkeys!** *Shh...Top Secret mission.*

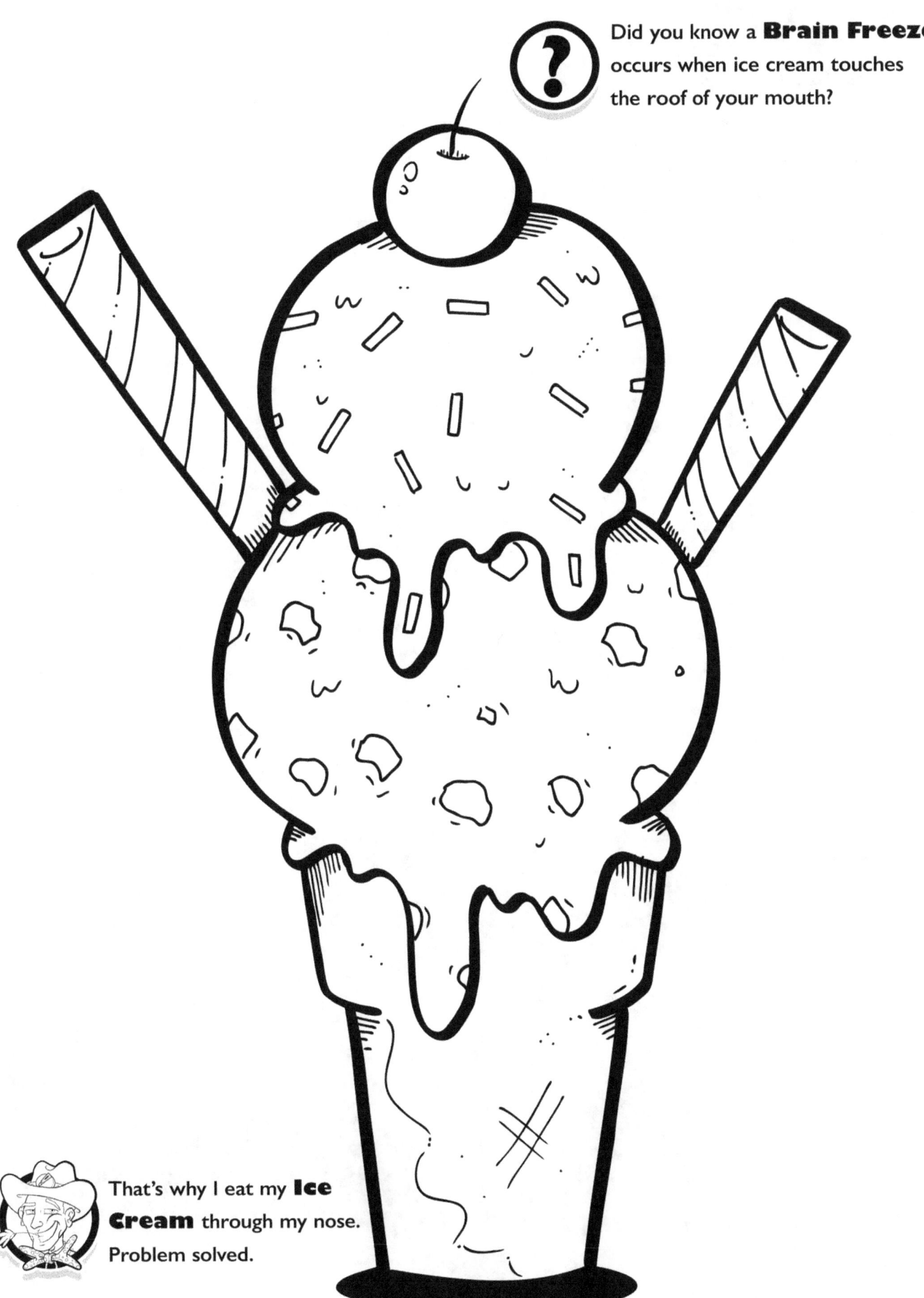

Did you know a **Brain Freeze** occurs when ice cream touches the roof of your mouth?

That's why I eat my **Ice Cream** through my nose. Problem solved.

? Did you know Americans eat roughly 8 billion **Chickens** every year?

I **wonder** how much of that is chicken tenders?

Did you know a **BLT Sandwich** consists of bacon, lettuce and tomato?

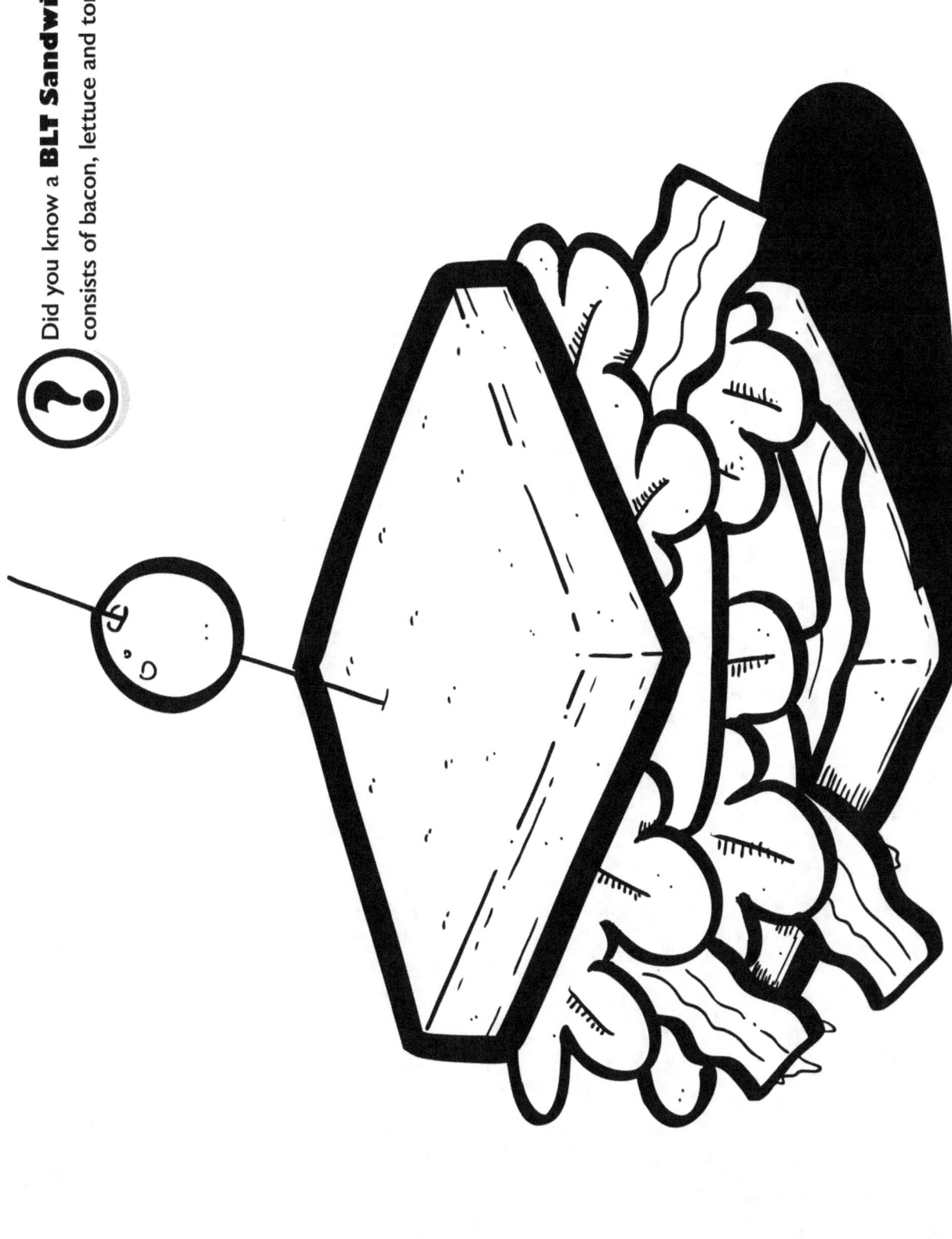

And here I've been making it wrong all these years!
I thought it was **Banana, Licorice and Tuna!**

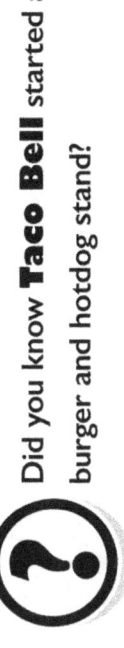

Did you know **Taco Bell** started as a burger and hotdog stand?

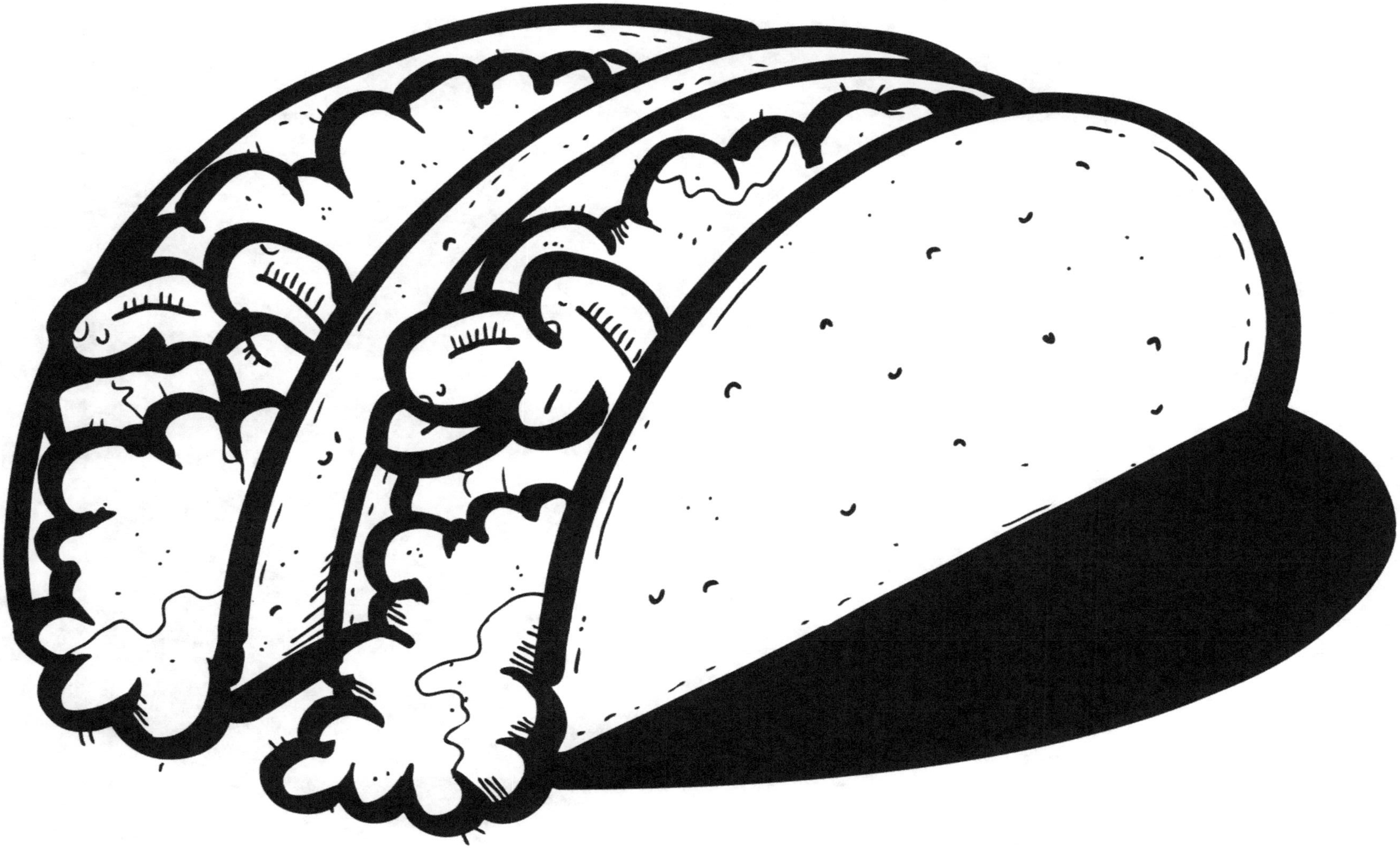

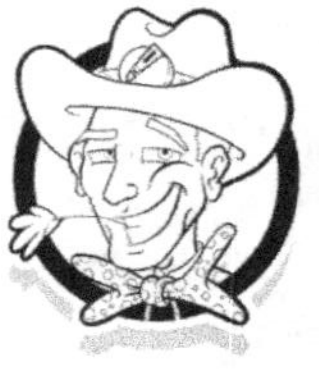

I wonder if **Burger King** started at a taco stand? Ha-Ha

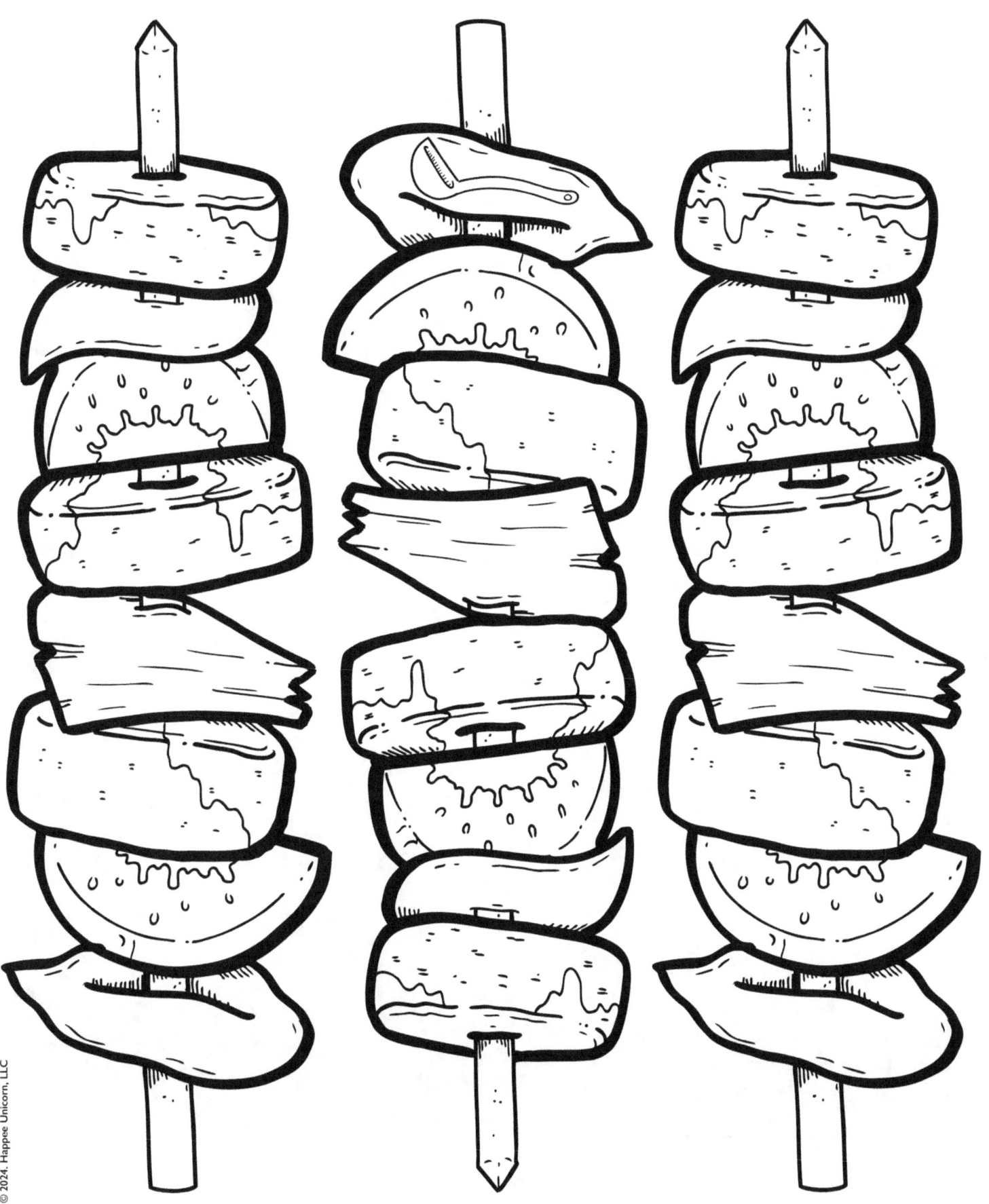

 Did you know **Colonel Sanders** opened his first restaurant inside of a gas station?

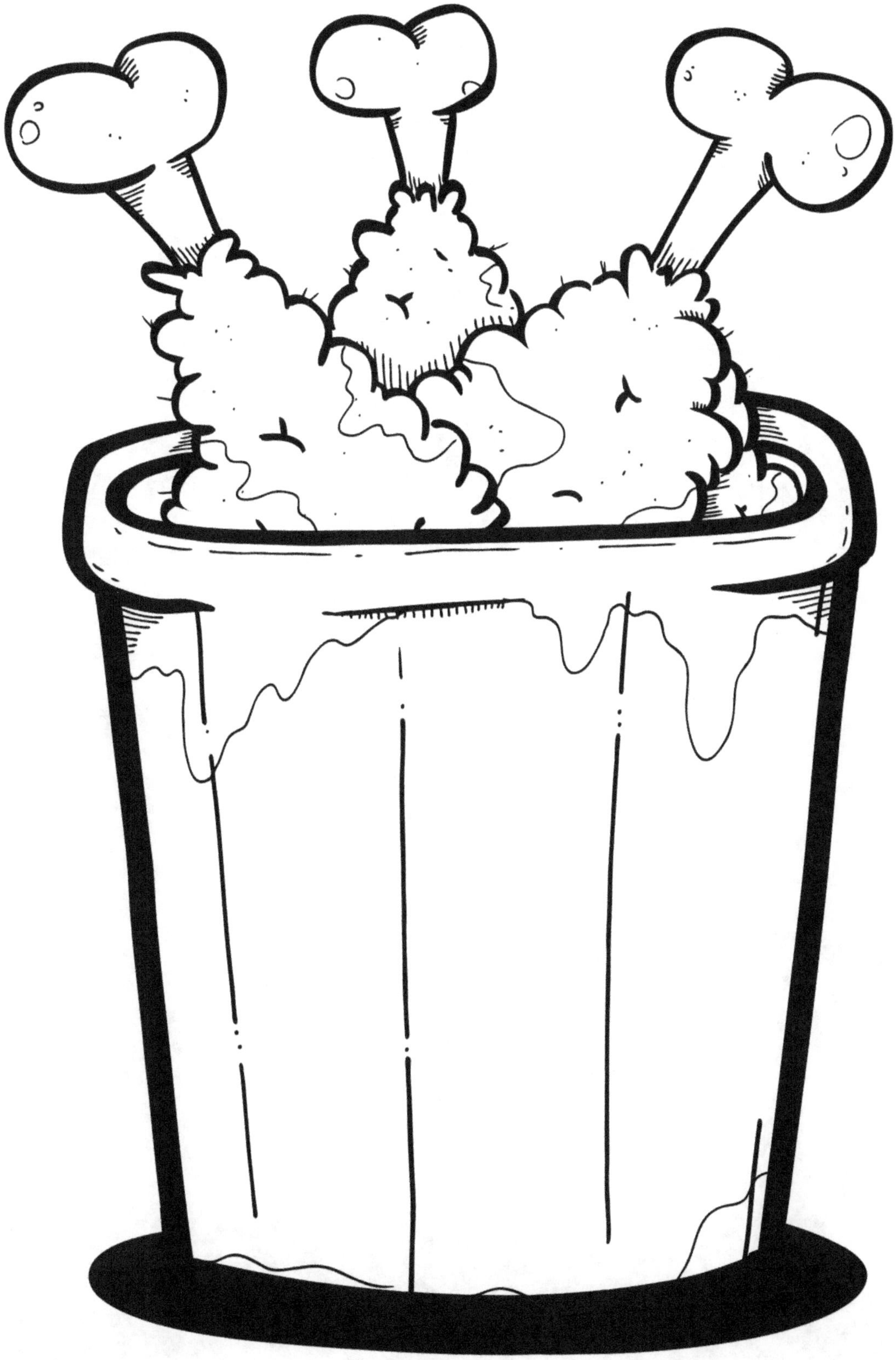

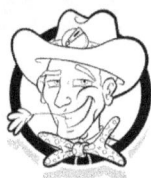 I wonder if they fried the chicken in **motoroil?**

Did you know it's believed that the very first **Apple Pie** was made in England over 600 years ago?

Mmmmm...warm apple pie with vanilla ice cream is the best!

How do you like your pie?

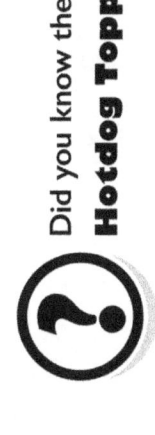

Did you know the most popular **Hotdog Topping** is mustard?

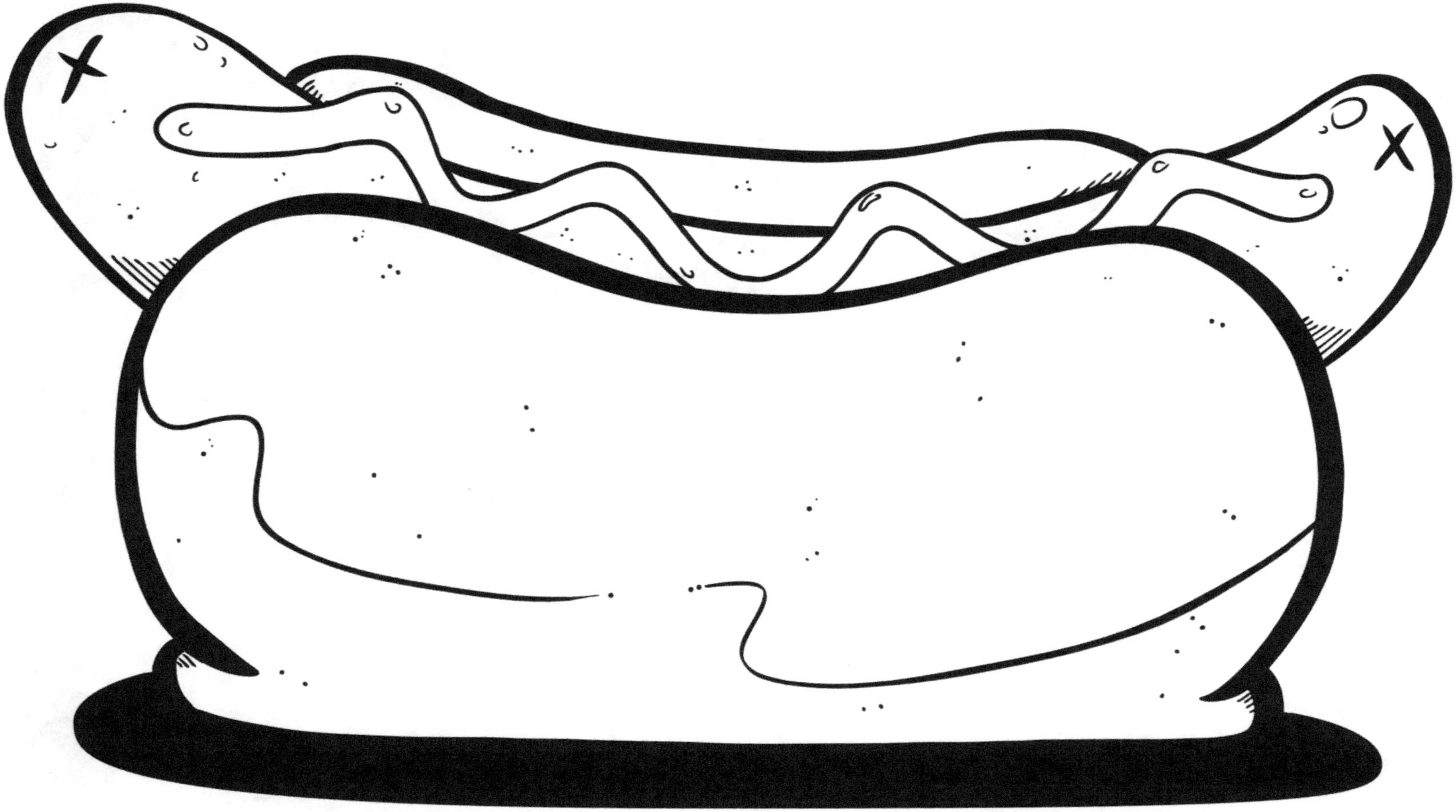

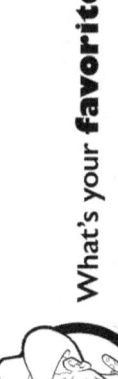

What's your **favorite** hotdog topping?

 Did you know that **Gyro** is probably one of the most mispronounced food names? It's not *jee-ros, jai-ros* or even *gee-ros*. The correct pronunciation is *Yeh-ro*.

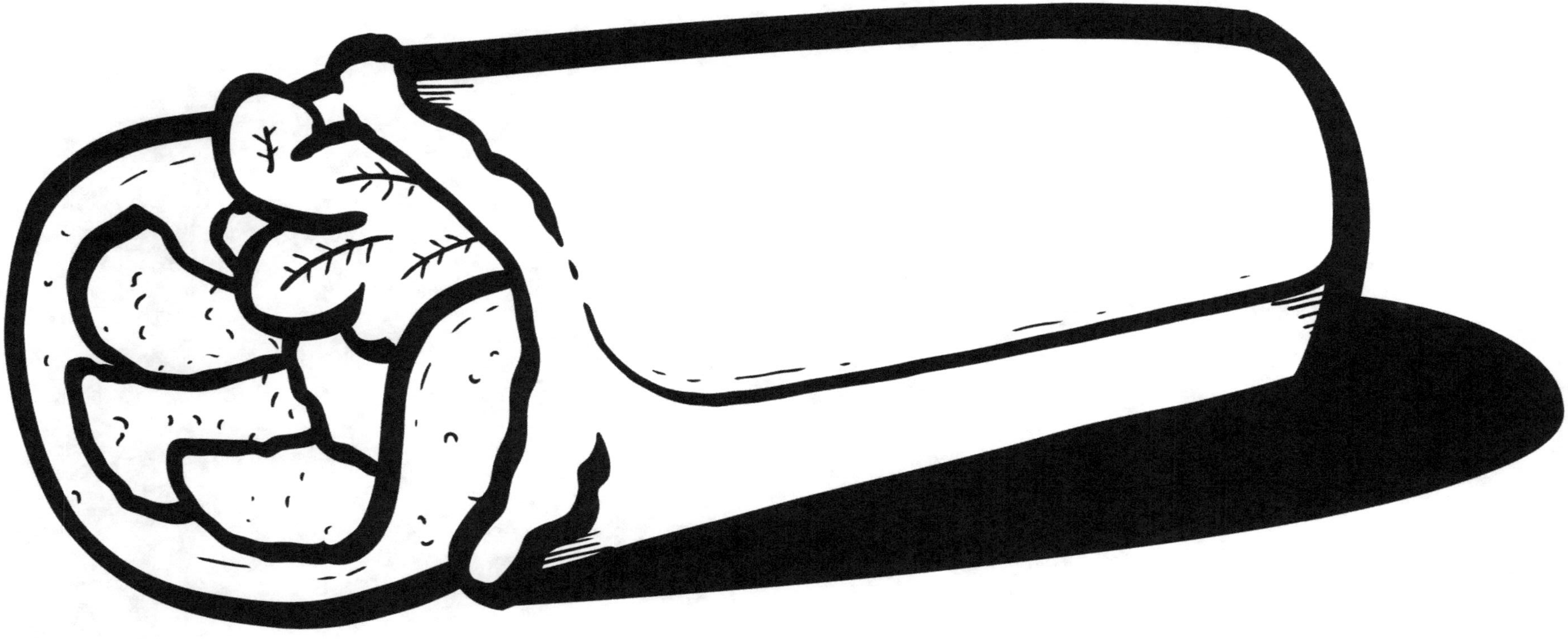

Gyro's are my all time **favorite** food!

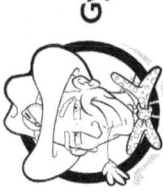

Did you know **Sloppy Joes** has many other names? Some include sloppy Jane, yum yums, slush burger and dynamite.

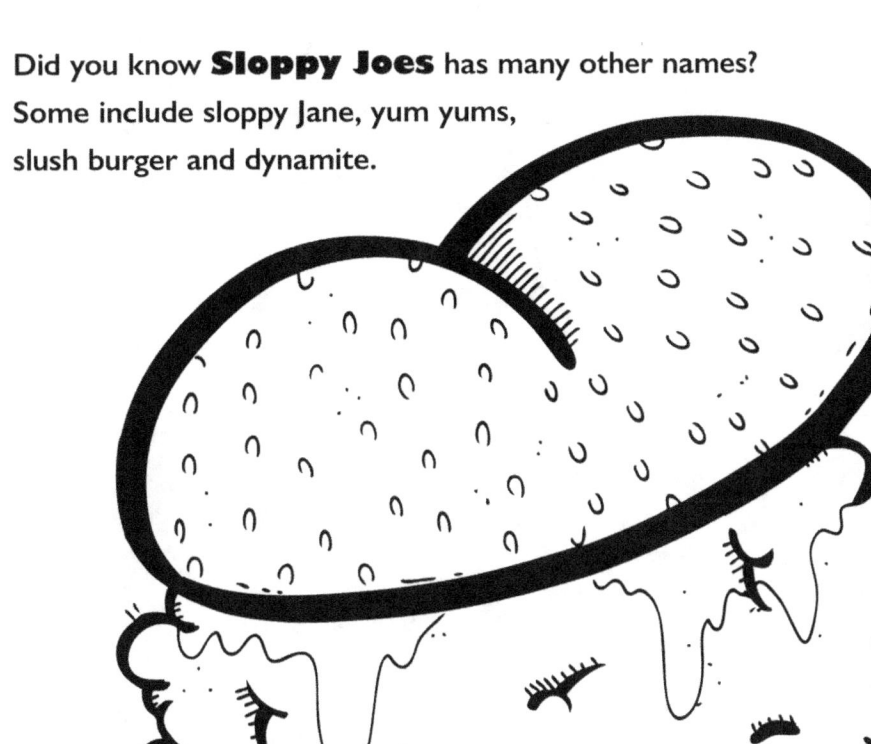

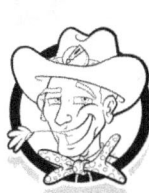

And here is my own addition;
Sloppy Slop Slops.

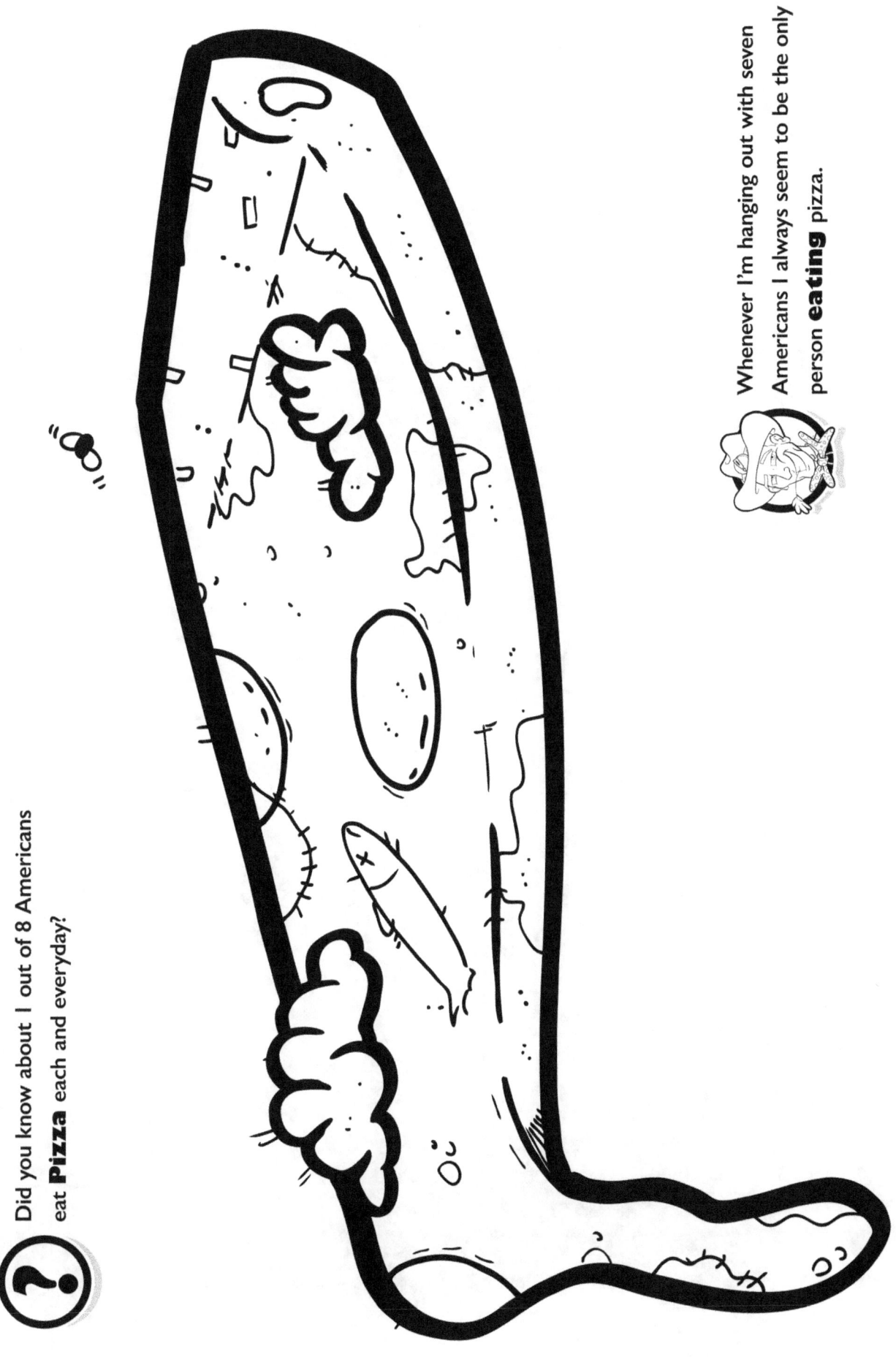

Did you know about 1 out of 8 Americans eat **Pizza** each and everyday?

Whenever I'm hanging out with seven Americans I always seem to be the only person **eating** pizza.

 Did you know the wrap of an **Egg Roll** is dipped in *egg or egg wash* before being deep-fried?

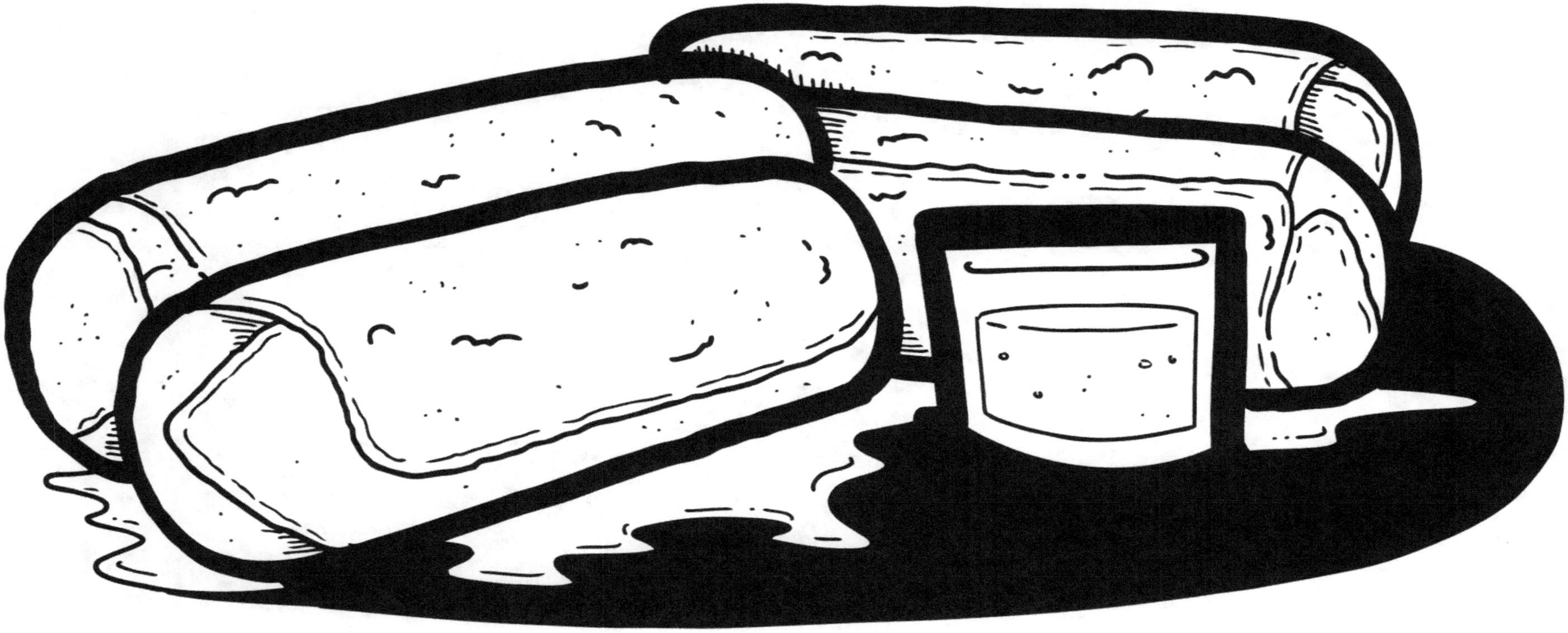

I **wonder** if that's why it's called an egg roll?

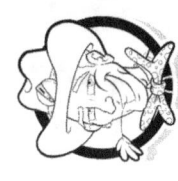

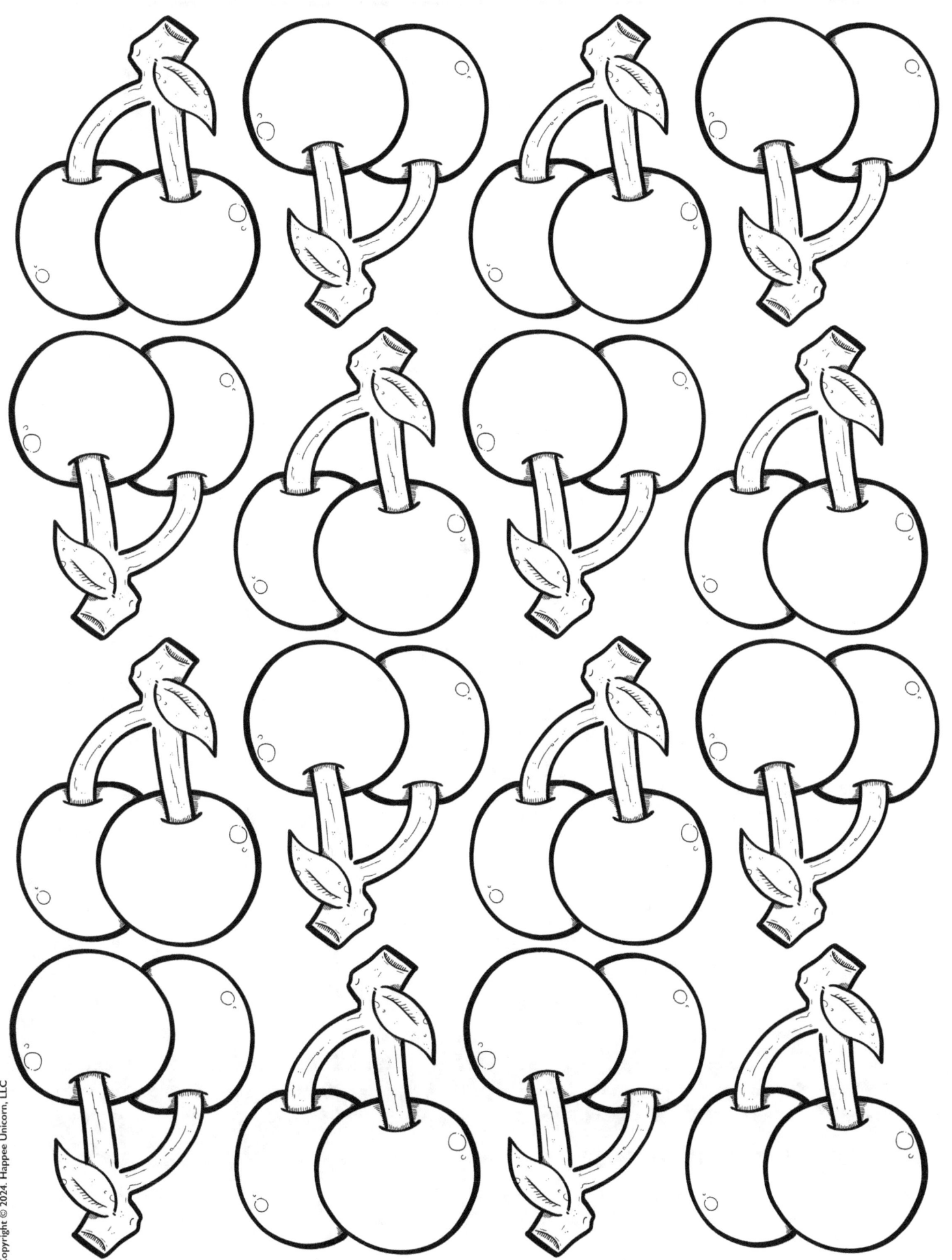

? Did you know the United States produces the most amount of **Blueberries** a year? Yup, nearly 240 thousand tons!

Whoa.

? Did you know **Kielbasa** is the Polish name for 'a sausage?'

I once ate Kielbasa everyday for almost a year! I was **obsessed.** Seriously.

? Did you know the world's most expensive

Steak costs $3,200?

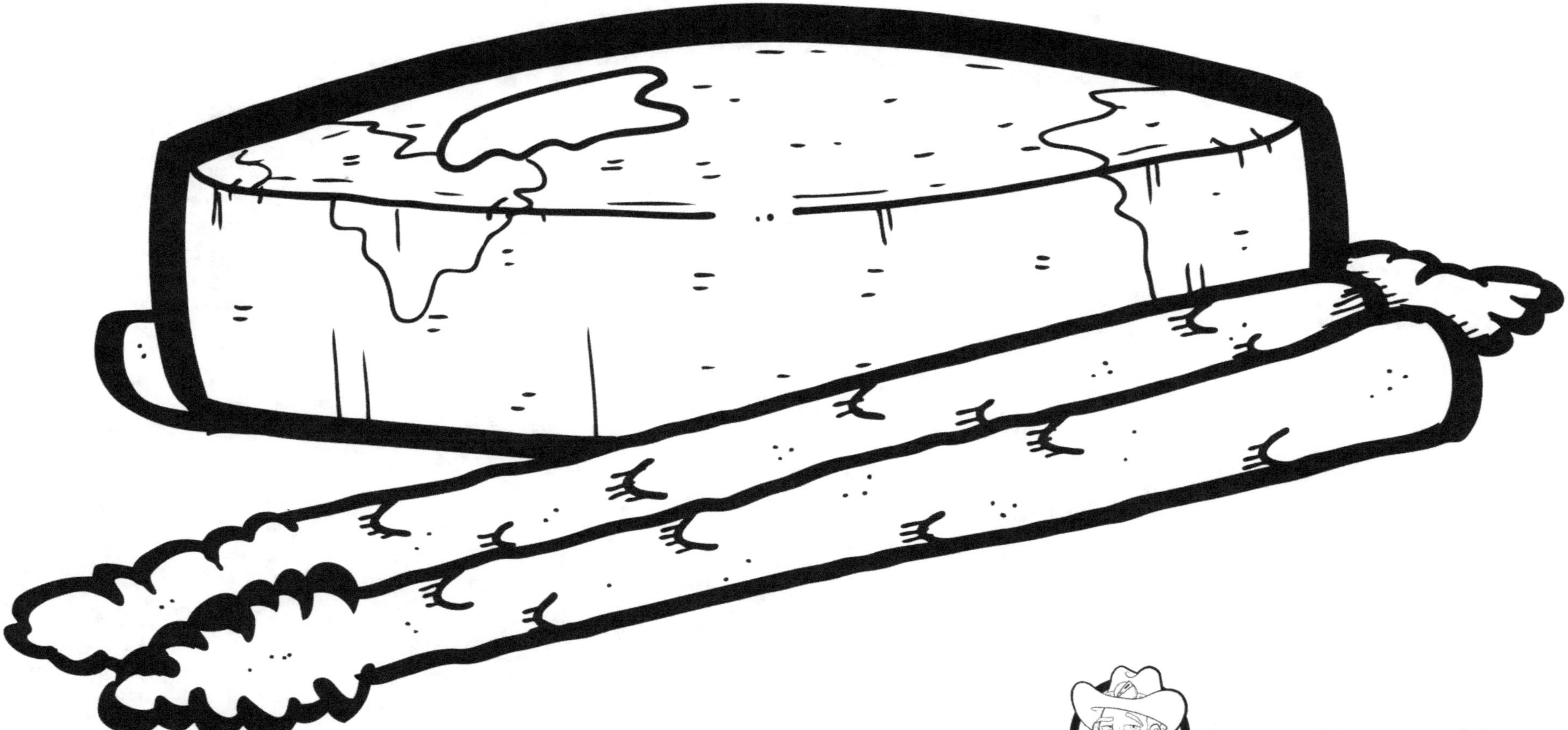

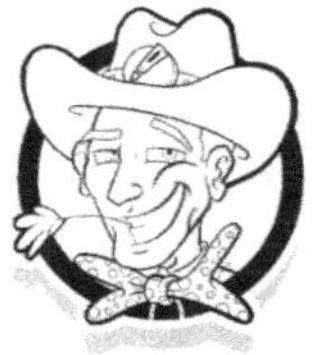

I wonder if there is **gold** inside?

 Did you know a **Watermelon** contains about 6 percent sugar and 92 percent water?

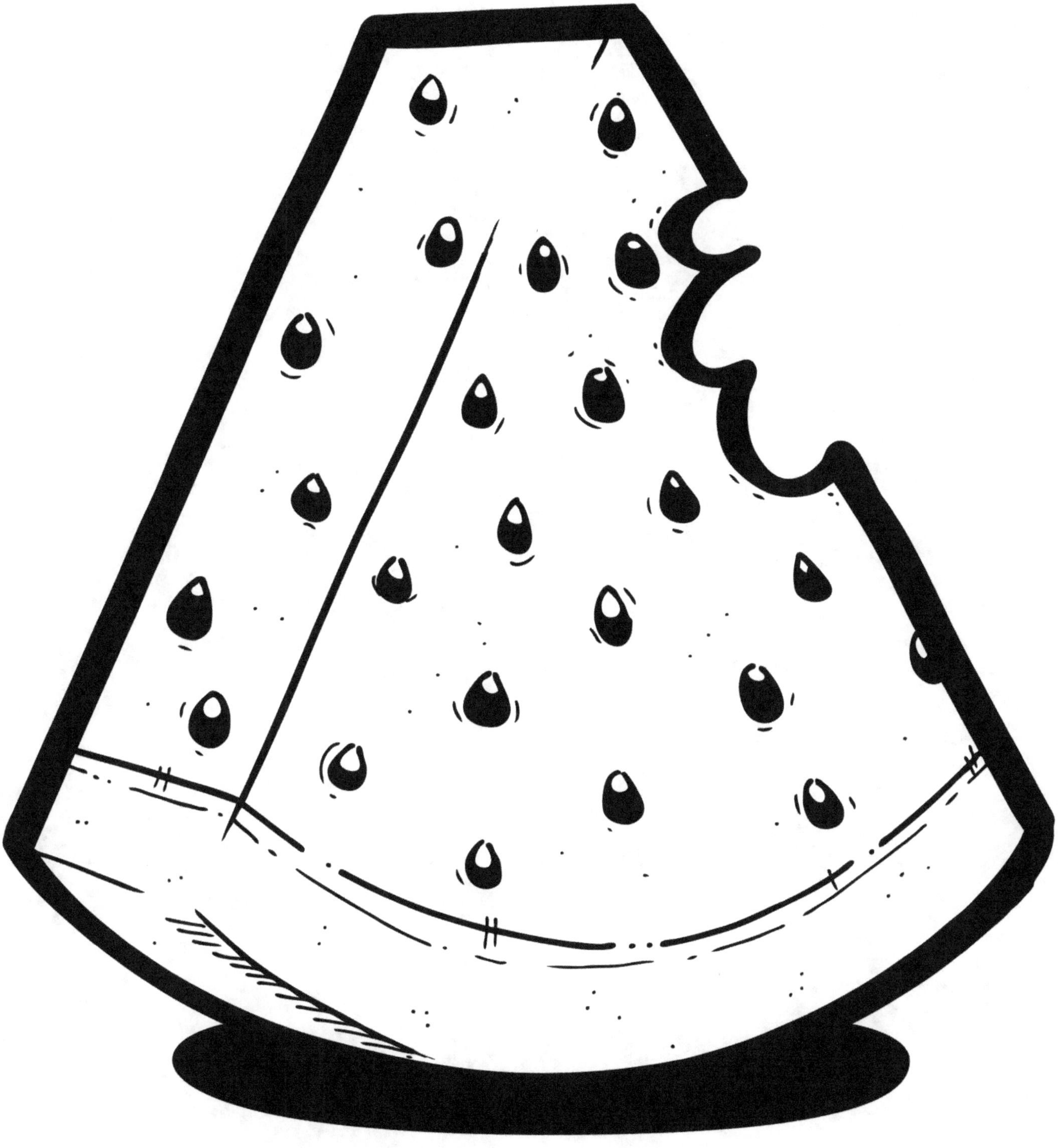

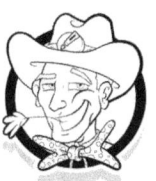 **Imagine** if it were reversed.

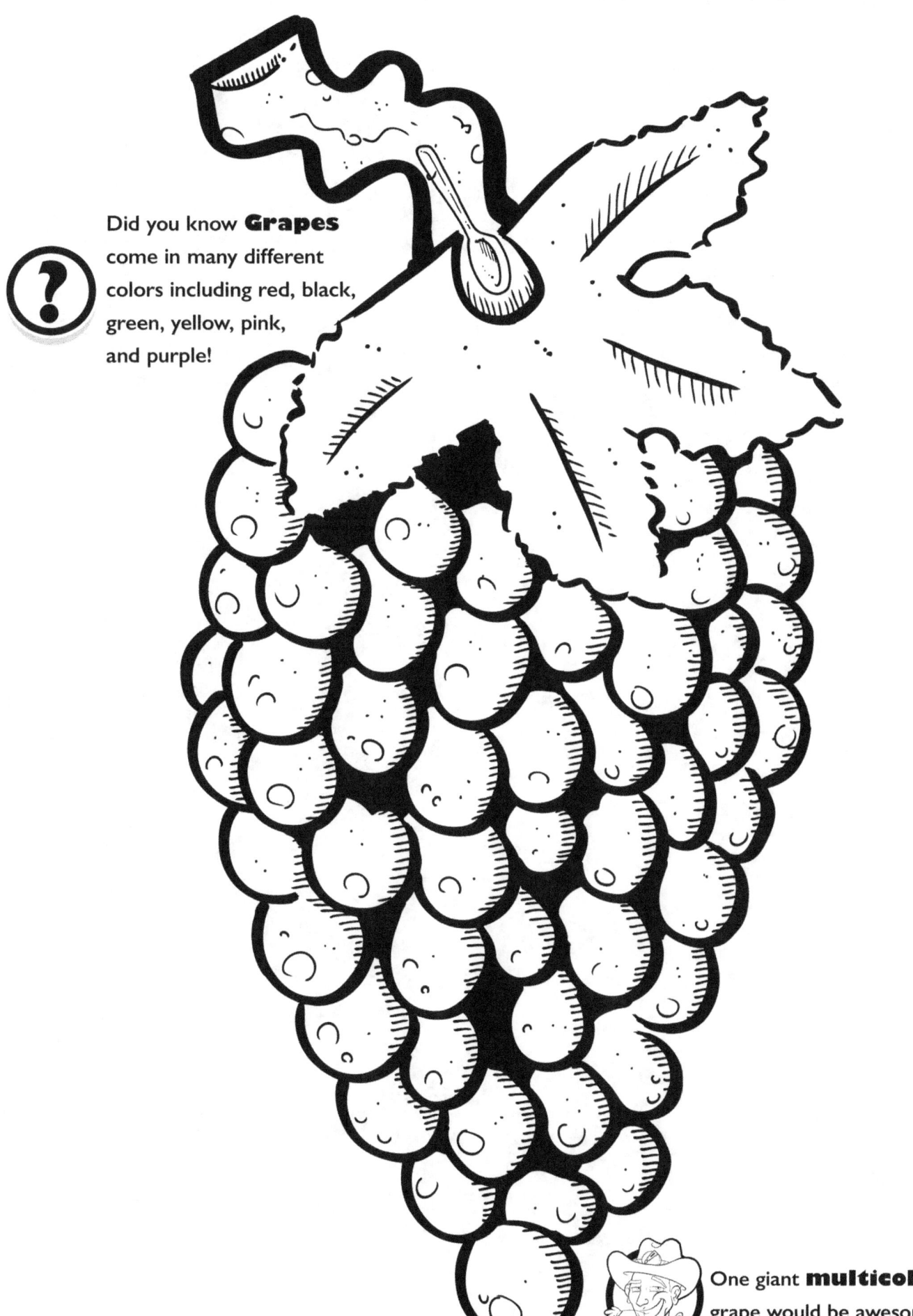

Did you know **Grapes** come in many different colors including red, black, green, yellow, pink, and purple!

One giant **multicolored** grape would be awesome!

Did you know there are over 2,000 varieties of **cheese** in the world?

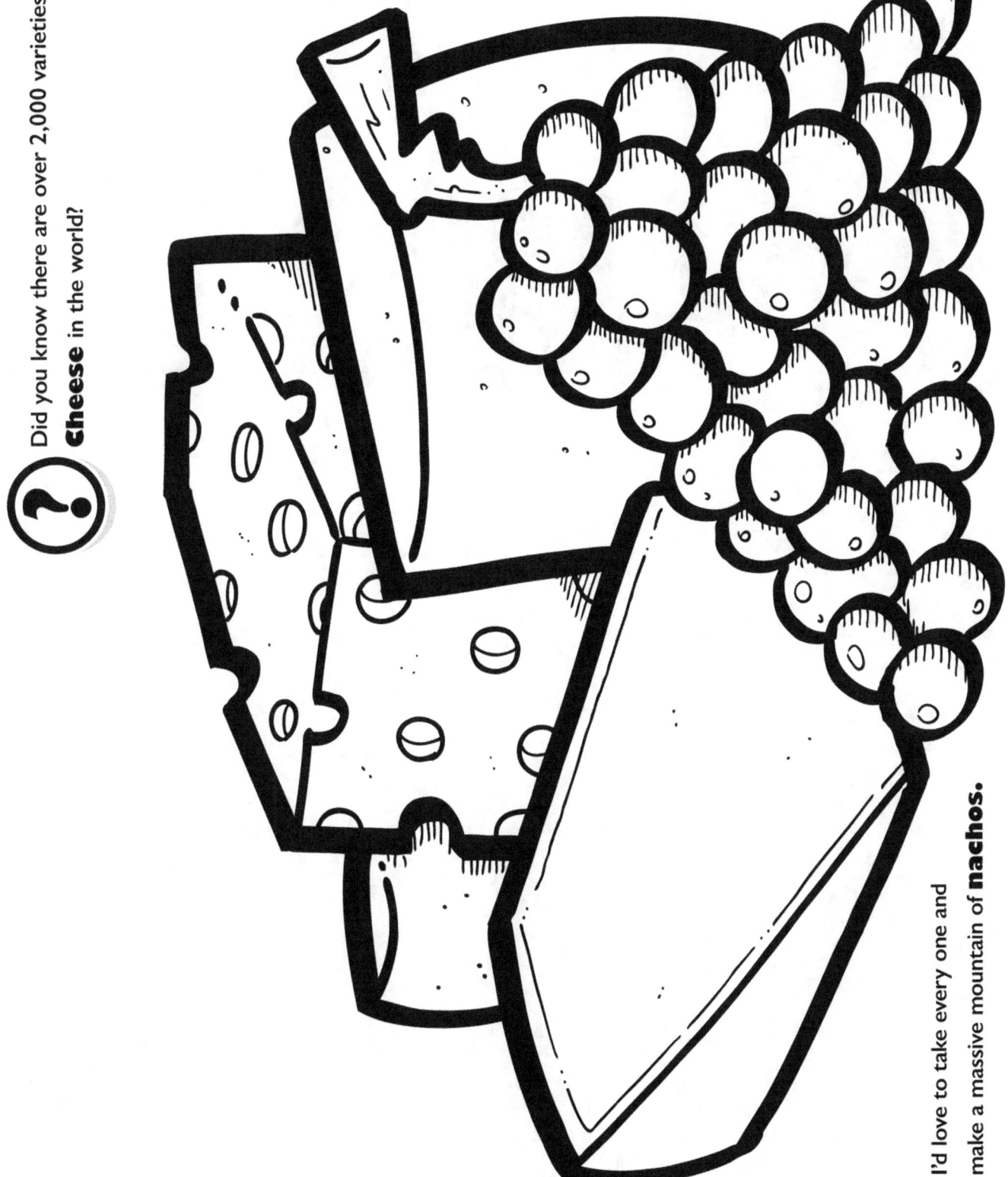

I'd love to take every one and make a massive mountain of **nachos.**

? Did you know the tradition of placing candles on a **Cake** is believed to have originated with the *Ancient Greeks?*

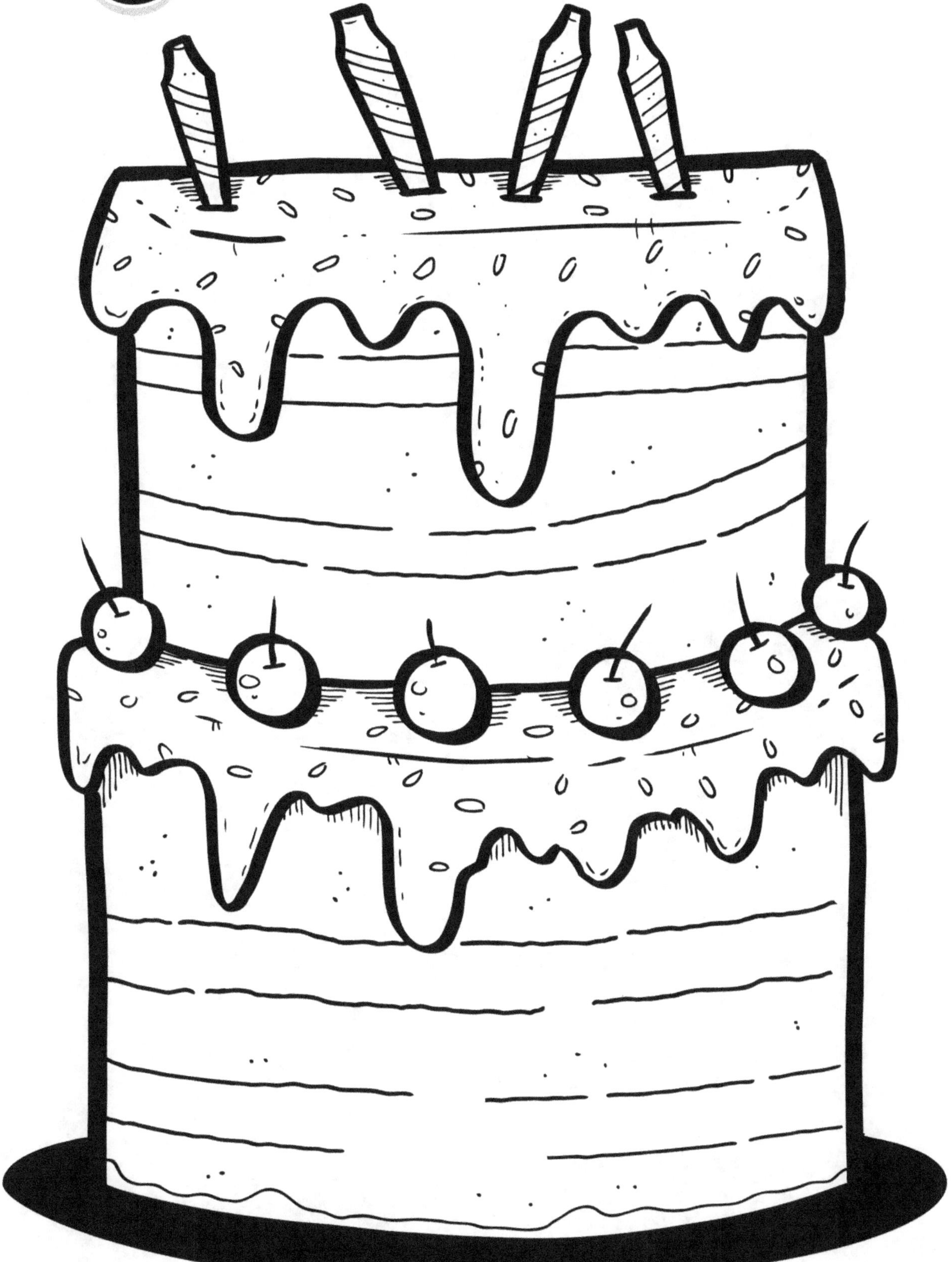

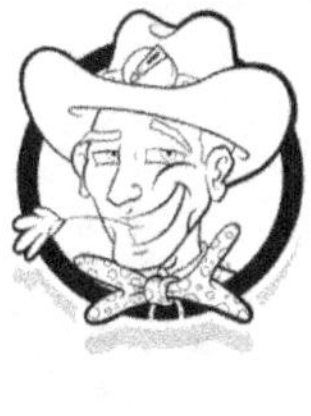

Don't forget to make a **wish!**

Fork - Pretzel Pattern Page

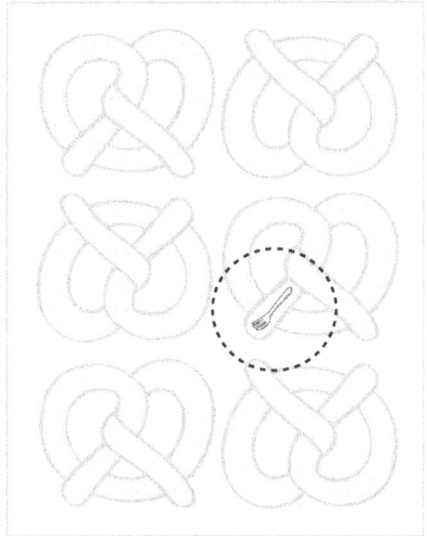

Inside the Pretzel

Chef Hat - Burrito

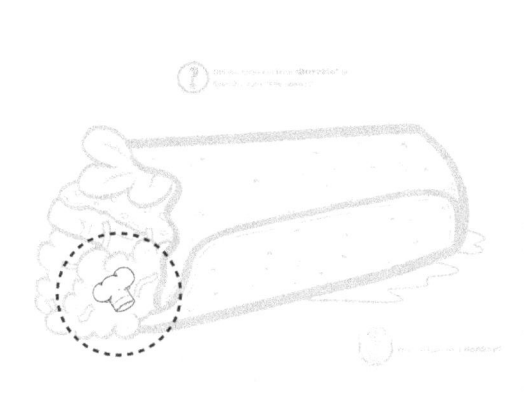

Inside Burrito Meat

Spoon - Grapes

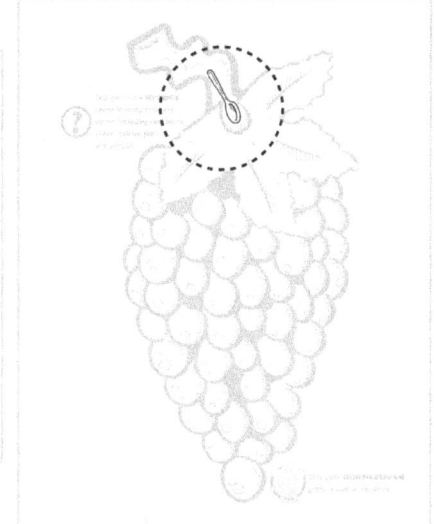

Inside the Stem

Knife - Sliced Fish

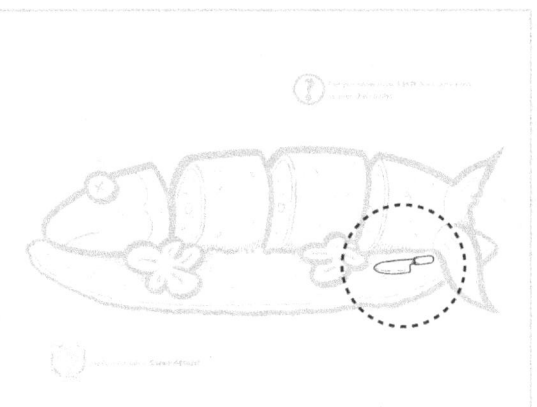

On Top of Rice

Mr. Gray's
Hidden Treasure
Answer Sheet

Oven Mit - Lobster

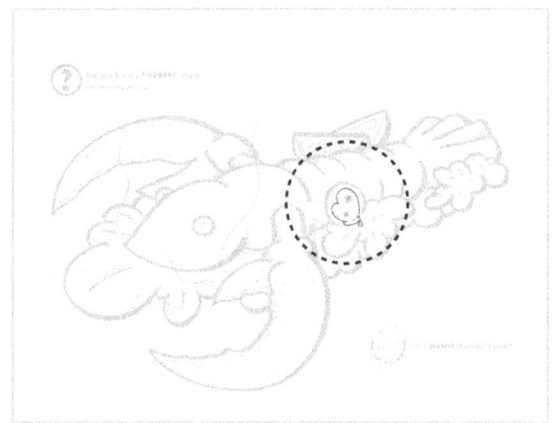

Inside Lettuce

Rolling Pin - French Fries

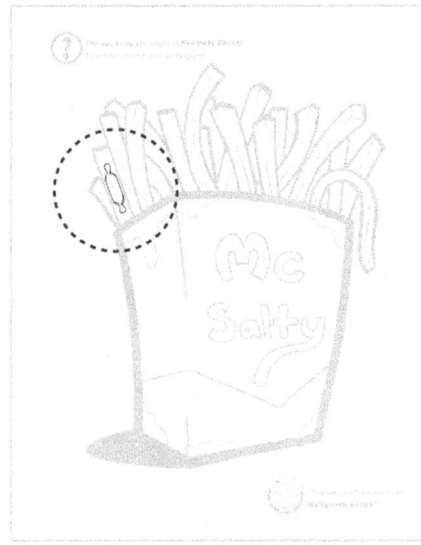

Inside French Fry

Spatula - Hard Taco

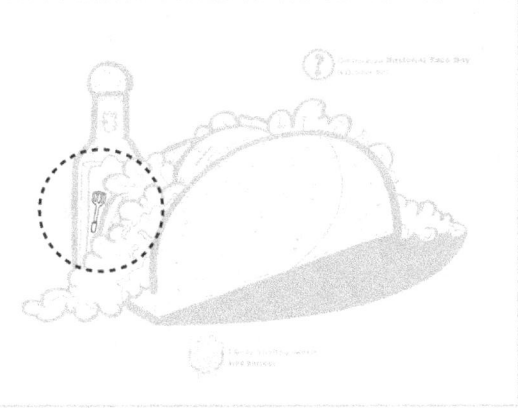

On The Bottle

Ladle - Kabob Pattern Page

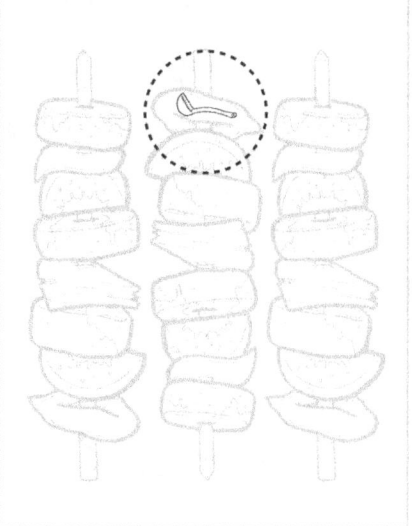

Top of Middle Kabob

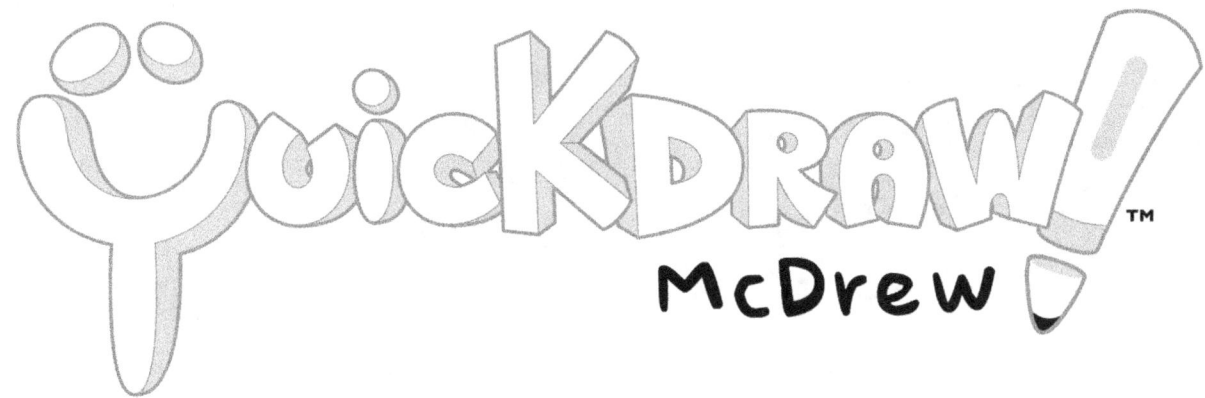

Howdy! My name is Mr. Gray, a.k.a. QuickDraw McDrew! The Fastest Cartoon Slinger in the West!™ I'm on a mission to awaken and strengthen the imagination that lives in all of us, because the truth is, imagination never truly dies. It just likes to play hide-n-seek from time to time, but I promise you it's still there. Like a baby riding a unicorn flying through space shooting planets with a booger gun! *(See, it's alive and well and we just need to find it.)* And together we will!

Your Wascally Cartoonist,

Mr. Gray

—Mr. G

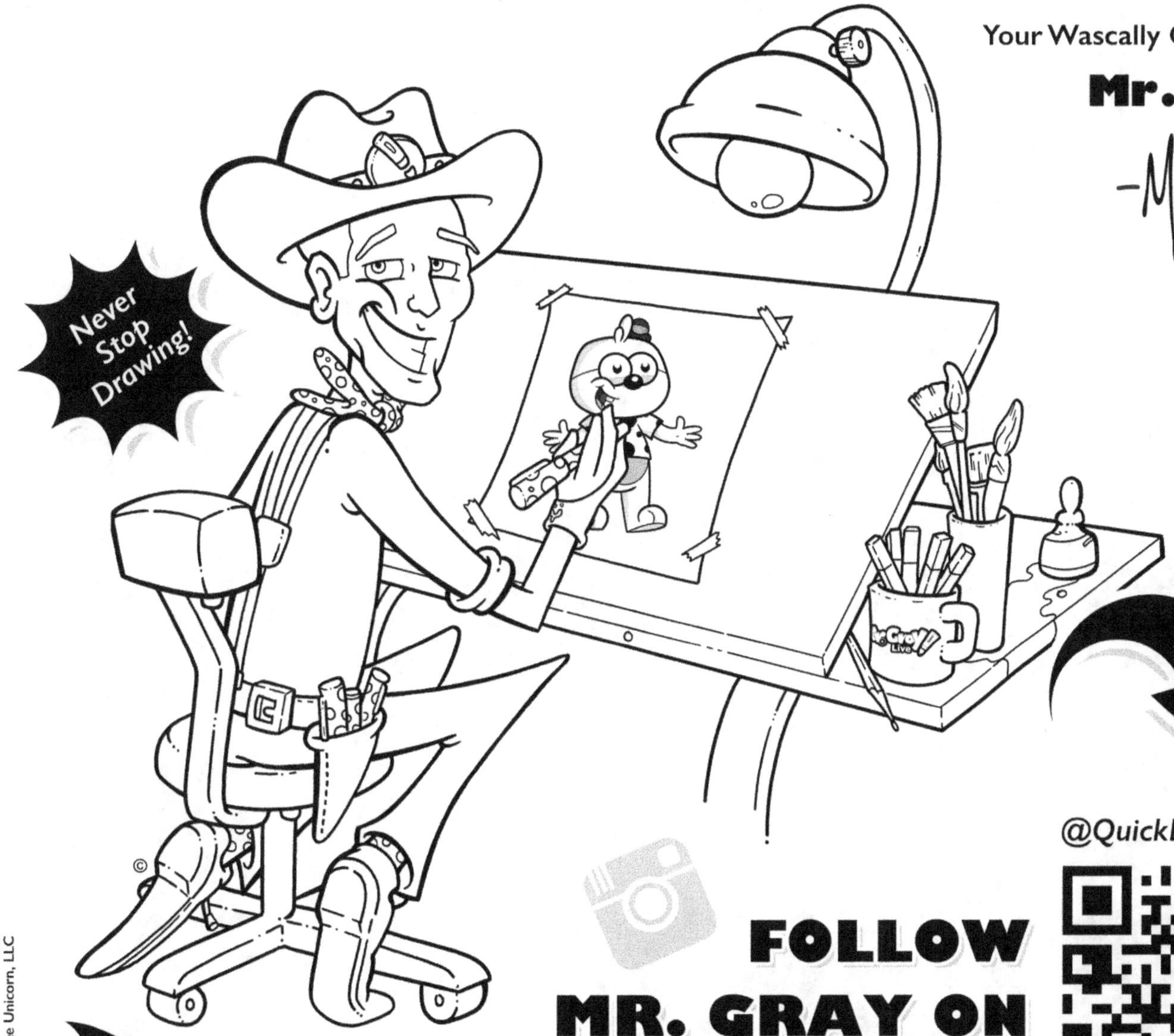

Never Stop Drawing!

@QuickDrawMcDrew

FOLLOW MR. GRAY ON INSTAGRAM

Write Mr. Gray:
Mr. Gray
P.O. Box 11711
Burbank, CA 91510

QuickDrawMcDrew.com

COLLECT THEM ALL!

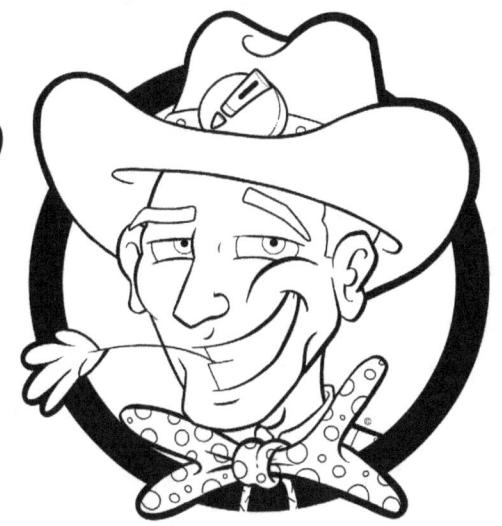

amazon.com
Prime

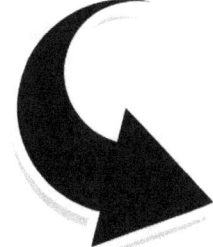

Mr. Gray's
ANIMAL
MASH UP!

Coloring Book | Volume One

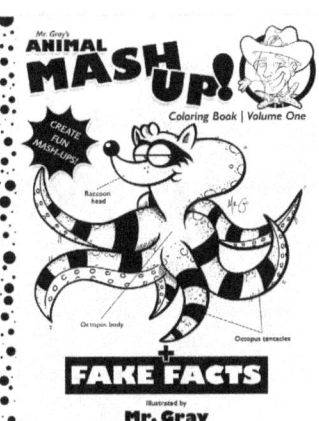

The
ANIMALS &FRIENDS

Coloring Book | Volume One

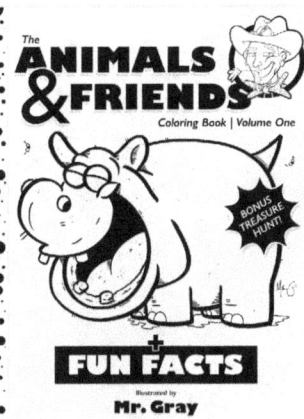

The
ANIMALS &FRIENDS

Coloring Book | Volume Two

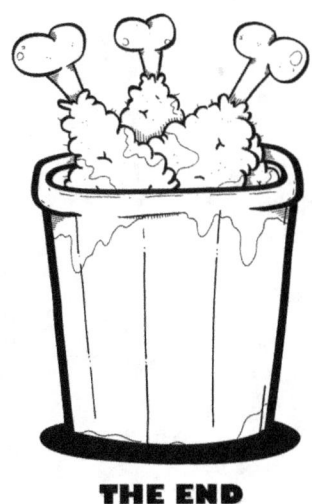

THE END

ISBN: 978-0-9988005-1-6

Second Edition. Printed by Amazon in the United States of America

Happee Unicorn, LLC - P.O. Box 11711, Burbank, CA 91510

Business Inquiries: mrgray@mrgrayart.com

www.mrgrayart.com